McAllister, Ian, 1969–
The Great Bear Sea :
exploring the marine lif
2013.
33305230237376
ca   11/05/13

D0702251

IAN MCALLISTER & NICHOLAS READ

THE GREAT BEAR SEA

EXPLORING THE MARINE LIFE OF A PACIFIC PARADISE

PHOTOGRAPHS BY IAN MCALLISTER

ORCA BOOK PUBLISHERS

Text copyright © 2013 Ian McAllister & Nicholas Read

All rights reserved. No part of this publication may be reproduced or transmitted in any
form or by any means, electronic or mechanical, including photocopying, recording or by any
information storage and retrieval system now known or to be invented, without permission
in writing from the publisher.

Library and Archives Canada Cataloguing in Publication

McAllister, Ian, 1969-
The Great Bear Sea : exploring the marine life of a Pacific paradise / Ian McAllister, Nicholas Read.

Includes bibliographical references and index.
Also issued in electronic format.
ISBN 978-1-4598-0019-9

1. Marine biology--British Columbia--Great Bear Sea--Juvenile
literature. I. Read, Nicholas, 1956- II. Title.

QH95.3.M33 2013   j578.7709164'33   C2013-901749-6

First published in the United States, 2013
Library of Congress Control Number: 2013934942

Summary: Explore the magnificent marine environment that exists on the remote central coast of British Columbia,
an area that has been called the Great Bear Sea.

*Orca Book Publishers is dedicated to preserving the environment and has
printed this book on Forest Stewardship Council® certified paper.*

Orca Book Publishers gratefully acknowledges the support for its publishing programs provided by the
following agencies: the Government of Canada through the Canada Book Fund and the Canada Council for the Arts,
and the Province of British Columbia through the BC Arts Council and the Book Publishing Tax Credit.

Design by Teresa Bubela
Cover images by Ian McAllister
Interior images by Ian McAllister except where otherwise noted
Page v map by D. Leversee, Sierra Club BC

About the photographs:
All of the images in this book are of wild animals in wild circumstances.
No digital manipulation or other alterations have taken place.

ORCA BOOK PUBLISHERS
PO Box 5626, Stn. B
Victoria, BC Canada
V8R 6S4

ORCA BOOK PUBLISHERS
PO Box 468
Custer, WA USA
98240-0468

www.orcabook.com
Printed and bound in Canada.

16 15 14 13 • 4 3 2 1

RIGHT: **Look beneath the
surface of the Great Bear
Sea and every color of the
rainbow awaits you.**

CONTENTS

The Great Bear Sea has many
moods, from placid to perilous.
If you catch it on a calm day,
it can be paradise.

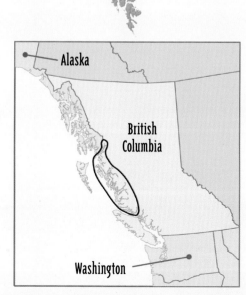

Great Bear Rainforest
British Columbia

Haida
Gwaii

Alaska

British
Columbia

Washington

Vancouver
Island

INTRODUCTION
Wild and Wet

What has an ocean got to do with a forest? The answer may surprise you: Everything.

When we look at a map of the Great Bear Rainforest, a vast and mysterious wilderness full of bears, wolves, cougars, mountain goats and deer, what we see first is the green. This area, about the size of the province of Nova Scotia, extends from the northern tip of Vancouver Island to the base of the Alaska Panhandle.

But that green—the part of the map that represents the rugged river valleys, the soggy bogs, the countless islands and the vast swaths of skyscraping trees—is only half the picture. The other half is blue, what conservationists now call the Great Bear Sea. And where the forest and sea meet is a constantly changing shoreline of rocky outcroppings, reefs, cliff faces,

LEFT: **The Great Bear Rainforest is fed and enriched by nutrients from the ocean. Ancient temperate rainforest with individual trees more than a thousand years old is common throughout the Great Bear Rainforest. Countless islands like these ones provide a buffer between the coast and the wild open ocean surf.**

MARITIME MORSELS

How big is the Pacific Ocean?

So big that it covers more than a third of the Earth's surface and contains more than half its water. So vast that if you put all the world's landmasses together in one place, the Pacific Ocean would be bigger. So enormous that if you grouped eighteen countries the size of the United States together, the Pacific would be bigger. It extends about 15,500 kilometers (9,600 miles) from north to south, and 19,800 kilometers (12,300 miles) from east to west. It is by far the biggest of the five oceans in the world. The others are (in order of decreasing size) the Atlantic, the Indian, the Southern and the Arctic.

RIGHT: **Estuaries like this one, where a river meets the ocean, are one of the most important habitats for both ocean- and land-dependent species. Salmon, wolves, bears, deer and many bird species depend on these critical habitats for their survival.**

beaches and estuaries, all connected to the Pacific, the largest and mightiest ocean in the world.

Make no mistake, the Great Bear *is* a forest—with trees as tall as the Capitol Building in Washington, DC. But it's fed, shaped and defined by that ocean. Year after year, storm after storm, the Pacific carries wind, rain and waves to the shores of the Great Bear. These storms are fierce and destructive, but it's thanks to them that rivers are full of water, estuaries thrive and nutrients are carried from the ocean floor to the forest, making the Great Bear one of the most diverse and bountiful havens for wildlife on the planet. It is also a place where indigenous people, or First Nations, have lived for more than ten thousand years.

But rich as the forests of the Great Bear are in bird and animal life, its marine environments are even richer. The waters off the forest's rugged coast contain more creatures than the forest itself—creatures that form the basis of food webs that extend all the way up to the great whales, the great bears and even the great trees. Some rainforest animals bridge these worlds by living part of their lives in the ocean and part of them on land, which goes to show how closely connected these worlds are.

But if we think we know the sea, we need to think again. What lies beneath that vast blue expanse is very much a mystery. In fact, it remains the least explored and least understood part of our planet.

What we do know is that life at sea and on land is inextricably linked. This book will explain how. Because, undoubtedly, without a Great Bear Sea to feed and nurture it, there would be no Great Bear Rainforest.

MARITIME MORSELS

What makes waves?

The force of the wind, the magnetic pull of the sun and the moon, the shifting of the Earth's crust, the passage of ships, water circulation caused by changing temperatures, and the depth of water at a particular point all contribute to the creation of waves. A wave begins when a number of factors like the ones described above shake up what would otherwise be an undisturbed area of water. As a strong wind tries to pull the water up, gravity and surface tension pull it down. This constant to and fro of forces causes water at the ocean's surface to rise and fall—first in ripples, then in waves.

RIGHT: **Just below the surface of the Great Bear Sea, an entirely new world exists. Full of color and exotic-looking life, intertidal zones like this one can support thousands of different species of plants and animals.**

CHAPTER ONE

Too Small to See

When we think about the Great Bear Rainforest, we usually think of trees and the animals living among them: the grizzly and black bears, the coastal wolves, the Sitka black-tailed deer, the eagles and the famous spirit bear, a bear with creamy white fur found only on BC's central coast. But even though they all live on land, they owe much of their well-being to creatures at sea—creatures so small you need a microscope to see them.

These creatures are called *plankton*, and the sea is full of them. So much so that plankton account for more than 90 percent of all life in the ocean. That's right, 90 percent of what scientists call *biomass*, meaning all the life—big, small, strong, weak, plant and animal— that exists in the ocean is composed of plankton.

LEFT: **Hooded nudibranchs cling to a kelp frond. These predatory sea slugs are found throughout the Great Bear Sea.**

MARITIME MORSELS

What do plankton look like?

They come in many different shapes and designs. One even resembles the lunar landing module that dropped Neil Armstrong onto the moon in 1969. Some have tails, which they use to whip themselves around the sea's surface. But most just let the sea take them where the sea chooses. Hence their name, plankton, which comes from the Greek word *planktos*, meaning "wandering" or "drifting."

When you stop to consider how many fish, whales and other creatures live there too, you'll realize what an astounding figure that is.

But without plankton those other creatures couldn't survive. When plankton photosynthesize (the process by which plants turn water, carbon dioxide, salt and light into tissue), they release oxygen into the water and eventually the air that rainforest bears and wolves (not to mention you) breathe. About 40 percent of all the photosynthesis on Earth is performed by plankton, meaning about 40 percent of all the world's oxygen is generated by creatures small enough to balance on the point of a pin.

There are two kinds of plankton: *phytoplankton*, which are plants, and *zooplankton*, which are animals. Zooplankton often eat phytoplankton and so become the basis of what are called *food webs*. When a little fish is eaten by a bigger fish, who's eaten by an even bigger fish or a marine mammal, that's a food web. This is how much of nature works. A killer whale eats a harbor seal who eats salmon who eat herring—who began the whole thing by eating plankton. Millions of them. Some people call this a "food chain," but life is more complex than a chain, so a "food web" is more accurate.

On any given day there are far too many plankton in the ocean for anyone to count. However, there are times when that already huge number gets even bigger—so big that the sea "blooms" with them. In the Great Bear Sea, the year's most important blooms occur in early spring when days get warmer and longer, and more light filters through the sea's surface.

The presence of this lighter, warmer water is a signal for plankton to multiply…and multiply and multiply. By March, each plankton cell divides into two new cells every day. Multiply that by the number of plankton at sea and you'll realize how an explosion of plankton can occur in no time. Within just three weeks, a single plankton cell can produce as many as a million offspring. So it isn't long before the Great Bear Sea becomes a kind of plankton soup. Some blooms grow so big they can be seen from space.

Often one kind of plankton will bloom before another. Then, when that species' life cycle is done, it will be followed by another and another. This way, spring blooms lead to summer blooms—like flowers. Spring snowdrops are followed by crocuses,

TOP: **Transparent and majestic nudibranchs are able to swim with small paddle-like flippers.**

MARITIME MORSELS

What's a red tide?

You may have heard the expression in relation to fishing. When a red tide is in place, it's dangerous to harvest shellfish like clams, mussels or crabs. Plankton are the reason. Some produce toxins that are poisonous to people—so poisonous that they can cause paralysis. So when these plankton bloom, toxins can build up in shellfish that eat them. These shellfish include geoduck (pronounced *goo-ey-duck*), clams, oysters, mussels, scallops, whelks and moon snails. And yes, because of the plankton's color, the sea, and therefore the tide, really does take on a red/brown hue.

daffodils and tulips. Summer roses precede lilies and dahlias. Plankton blooms are the same. Depending on the time of year and the kind of plankton, plankton blooms can turn the sea red, then orange, then burgundy, then white.

However, regardless of their appearance, it's their ecological significance that makes them so important. It's no exaggeration to say that without plankton and the food and oxygen they supply, the world would be profoundly different.

Looking around at the tall trees in the Great Bear Rainforest, it's hard to imagine that they owe so much to something as tiny as plankton. But they do. Someone once said good things come in small packages. Whoever it was wasn't kidding.

RIGHT: **No, it's not an alien or a space shuttle that's lost its way. Instead, *Pandeidae hydromedusa* is one of many species of ocean plankton found in the Great Bear Sea. Plankton form the basis of a food web that extends all the way up to the great whales.**

PHOTOGRAPH BY MARIE-JOSÉE GAGNON

FAR RIGHT: **Canada's west coast contains most of the world's remaining intact temperate rainforest.**

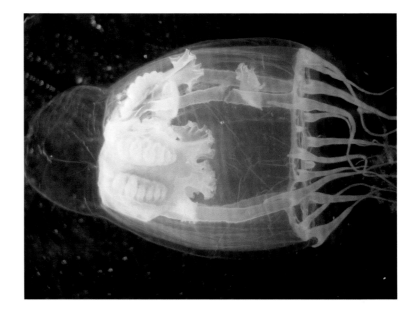

CHAPTER TWO

Something Fishy

"There's always more fish in the sea." People use this expression when someone's had his or her heart broken. The idea is that, just as there are always more fish in the sea, there's always another man or woman to meet and perhaps fall in love with. Obviously, whoever coined the expression had no idea that a day would come when many of the world's fish species were disappearing, including those in the Great Bear Sea. But the metaphor does speak to how we once thought the oceans would produce fish forever.

More than 30,000 fish species live in the world's oceans, and so far we know of only about 325 that navigate the waters of the northeast Pacific. But they range from the finger-sized northern anchovy (pizza, anyone?) to the elephantine Pacific basking shark,

LEFT: **Highly territorial and equipped with poisonous spines, this quillback rockfish can live to be a hundred years old—providing a predator doesn't eat it first.**

a very rare salt-water giant that can grow to be 12 meters (40 feet) long and weigh 6,350 kilograms (7 tons).

Another seventy or so species live in BC's fresh-water lakes and rivers. But a few really exceptional fish live in both. They include the rainforest's five species of salmon and its steelhead trout. These fish are *anadromous*, meaning they're born in fresh water, live most of their lives at sea, but return to rivers and streams to lay their eggs. Sturgeon, smelt, striped bass and eulachon (pronounced *oo-la-kin*) are also anadromous. Meanwhile, some eel species (long snake-like fish whose lack of hind fins enables them to wriggle through rocky reefs) are *catadromous*, meaning they're born at sea, live most of their lives in lakes and rivers, and then return to the sea to spawn.

BOTTOM: **Large-net seine fisheries have caused local herring populations to collapse in many parts of the Great Bear Sea.**

When you talk about a fish's life, you're talking mainly about three things: 1) searching for food and mates; 2) swimming with or against tides and currents; and 3) avoiding becoming someone else's dinner. The sea can be one dangerous place. Everywhere you turn there's someone or something else—another fish, seal, sea lion, killer whale or fisherman—with only one thing on his mind: his stomach. An adult orca eats up to 4 percent of its body weight each day. That's more than 140 kilograms (300 pounds) of salmon, seals, cod or herring between one morning and the next. An adult Steller sea lion is even more ravenous. It eats 6 percent of its 1,500-pound body weight each day. Human beings are no slouches either. In an average year, more than 150 million kilograms (165,000 tons) of fish are caught by commercial fishermen along the BC coast. Add it all up, and that's one heck of a lot of fish being chased, caught, swallowed and digested.

This dog-eat-dog, or fish-eat-fish, world is the reason so many smaller fish species like salmon, herring and trout lay so many eggs. A single salmon can lay up to 7,000 eggs at one go. They have to because nature has fixed it so that when a salmon, herring or trout pair produces a clutch of eggs (the female lays the eggs and the male fertilizes them), it's likely that only two of those eggs will ever grow up to reproduce. The rest are eaten or destroyed.

What defines a fish? The answer to that question is not as cut-and-dried as you may think. Almost all fish, except tuna and mackerel, are cold-blooded. That means their body temperature is determined by their environment. So when the surrounding water is cold,

MARITIME MORSELS

How do fish eat?

Needless to say, fish eat through their mouths, like people. But the position of a fish's mouth depends on the fish. So does the number and placement of their teeth. Teeth can be present on a fish's upper and lower jaws, on the roof of its mouth and even on its tongue. Fish use these tongue teeth to hold food steady in preparation for swallowing it. Some fish, including minnows and suckers, have teeth in their throats, which they use to further break up food.

MARITIME MORSELS

What is a hagfish?

Hagfish, another mysterious fish of the Great Bear's deep waters, have been around for about 500 million years and are one of our best links to a distant past. This eel-like fish has eyes under its skin, can shed a gallon of slime to help distract predators, can tie itself into a knot, and will burrow into the carcasses of dead animals in order to eat them from the inside out.

so are most fish. They also breathe through a system of gills, and almost all fish are *vertebrates*, meaning they have a backbone. Animals without backbones—plankton, for example—are *invertebrates*.

What about scales? Don't all fish have scales? No. Sharks, for example, are covered in small streamlining enamel plates, while sculpins (a small prehistoric-looking shallow-water fish common in the Great Bear Rainforest) have prickles on their heads and fins. Nor do all fish have fins. Think of eels. Jaws? Nope. Hagfish (see the sidebar) and lampreys (which look more like hoses than fish) have no jaws or spines. Yet they're fish too, and they look nothing like the heroes of *Finding Nemo*.

The exception to this rule are octopuses, which are also plentiful in the Great Bear Sea. They are not fish; they're mollusks. The giant Pacific octopus, which lives along the northern edge of the Pacific from British Columbia to Japan, is the largest octopus species in the world with a reach of up to nine and a half meters, or thirty-one feet.

All of which goes to show what a general term *fish* is. Yet it's the best we have for such a rich and varied group of animals.

In the Great Bear Sea most fish live at shallow or moderate depths, where enough light filters through the water for plants and plankton to grow. Most are active during the day, though some come out only at night. These fish sink to deeper parts during the day to rest and avoid predators. Meanwhile, a few others, such as the lantern fish, remain out of sight all the time. Lantern fish are tiny fish (two to twelve

centimeters long, depending on the species) only a strand up from plankton on the food web. They get their name from the light-producing organs on their bodies that can light up the sea in shades of blue, green or yellow (depending on the species and sex) like…well, lanterns.

Regardless of their peculiarities, however, what you can say about all fish is that they know how to swim. Most have sleek, streamlined bodies that enable them to move through water like an arrow through the air. Why do you think torpedoes, submarines and sailboats look the way they do—rounded at the nose and tapered at the tail? Because this fish shape lends itself so well to slicing through water.

However, if a fish spends most of its time closer to the sea's bottom foraging for food, its body tends to be flatter. Think of flounder, halibut and sole. Their body

TOP: **In the Great Bear Sea, most fish, like these tube-snouts, live at shallow or moderate depths where enough light filters through for plants and plankton to grow.**

shapes make turning easier, and their color allows them to blend into the ocean bottom. Sometimes all you can see is one little black eye poking out of the mud, but that eye could be attached to a 300-pound halibut!

With the exception of the truly extraordinary salmon (more about them in Chapter Three), no one species of fish is more important than another in the Great Bear Sea. Each fills its own important ecological niche. Nevertheless, some feature more prominently than others.

Included among these is that twelve-meter, 6,350-kilogram basking shark, the second-largest fish in the world. Only the whale shark is larger. Several other shark species—including the blue, the six-gill and the Pacific angel shark, which, thanks to its broad, flat head and body looks more like a ray than a shark—call the northeast Pacific home too.

On the other side of the scale, there are those Pacific herring. They may not be much to look at (typically thirty centimeters, or just shy of a foot, long and

MARITIME MORSELS

Can fish see and hear?

Experiments suggest that most fish can distinguish colors, and many are thought to have excellent vision. But given the limited amount of light underwater, they probably don't see much except when they're near the surface. Fish don't have ears, but they do have internal organs that resemble ears, one on either side of their head. These organs help fish maintain their balance the way our inner ears help keep us steady. They may help them hear too, though we can't know without being fish ourselves.

FAR LEFT: **This red Irish lord relies on its incredible camouflage to hide from predators.**

LEFT: **Fishermen haul in a net of wild salmon, once one of the main economic drivers of the Great Bear Sea. Today many salmon stocks are in decline because of overfishing, habitat destruction and fish farming.**

MARITIME MORSELS

Do fish sleep?

Not in the way we do, but they certainly do rest. Some fish will bury themselves in sand or hide themselves in crevices, where they become still—so still that you can pick them up. Some fish, however, such as sharks, have to swim continuously to keep breathing. But even they appear to shut down from time to time. That is, they keep moving while using the ocean as a great big waterbed.

RIGHT: **Seabirds like these double-crested cormorants are also an integral part of the Great Bear Sea. When fish school in large numbers below the sea's surface, seabirds plunge in to feast on them.**

bluish green and silvery in color), but the Great Bear Sea wouldn't be the same without them.

Herring are miraculous. Early in spring, just as the winter snow is melting, they swim to the coast in vast schools, measured in thousands upon thousands of tons. Then, when conditions are right, females begin laying eggs—up to 20,000 per fish. When males discharge milt or sperm over these eggs, there's so much of it that the ocean turns white. The result is a harvest of fertilized pearl-like eggs that stick to eel grass, kelp and other underwater plants for two to three weeks while the herring embryos develop. Then, voilà! Millions of tiny herring appear to start the cycle all over again.

That is, if they get the chance. Even before any eggs are laid, eagles, cormorants and loons will swoop down to attack the spawning adults. Then so many gulls arrive to pick over the carcasses that the sky turns almost white. No wonder. For many rainforest species this is the first easy meal of the year. Below the sea's surface, rockfish emerge from their inky dark hiding places to eat the eggs, while along the forest's rocky shore, bears and wolves appear to pick at them at low tide. Even humpback whales, fresh from their Hawaiian nursing grounds, vacuum them up in their huge barrel mouths.

Herring are so plentiful, and so many species—including humans—feed on them, that they're known as a "foundation" species, meaning they're one of the foundations on which the entire Great Bear Rainforest ecosystem is built. Imagine removing the concrete foundation from your house. Think what would happen.

The same kind of disaster would happen to the coastal sea and forest if herring disappeared.

The Pacific sand lance, a silvery knife blade of a fish, is even smaller than the herring, but its impact on the rainforest is just as big. Only fifteen centimeters or six inches long, and only a couple of centimeters in diameter, a single sand lance doesn't amount to much. But like the herring's, its ecological significance is immense. The northeast Pacific teems with sand lance (schools of them glitter like underwater disco balls). Good thing too, given that most coastal sea birds and many larger fish—including herring, cod, pollock and salmon—eat them.

It's the same with sardines. When you hear the word, you probably think of blue-green fish the size of your finger squashed side by side in a tin. But before

BOTTOM: **First Nations people from the Knight Inlet area, the southern part of the Great Bear Rainforest, process eulachon, a small oily fish once abundant in the Great Bear Sea, to make "grease." Eulachon grease is traditionally one of the most treasured commodities as a trade item and an important source of vitamins.**

they were packed like sardines, they were swimming freely in the sea and feeding on plankton. Sardines may be small, but like herring and Pacific sand lance, their place in the ocean's food web is crucial because so many larger marine species eat them. Species such as Pacific cod, which are then eaten by marine mammals and people.

Eulachon were harvested by coastal First Nations long before European immigrants arrived. They're eaten fresh, smoked or dried. Eulachon oil, rich in vitamin D, is often used by First Nations as a condiment in meals and as a component of their traditional medicines. The dried fish itself also can be lit like a candle. At sea, eulachon are eaten by halibut, sturgeon, dogfish and salmon, while spawning eulachon provide a ready river-catch each spring for rainforest bears and birds.

TOP: **Herring may not look like much, but this foundation species supports the entire ecosystem of the Great Bear Sea. Of course, these gulls just find them delicious.**

MARITIME MORSELS

How do gills work?

Gills are located on either side of a fish's head and are covered with gill covers. A gill consists of a bony arch supporting a number of filaments filled with blood vessels. When a fish opens its mouth and draws water inside its body, the water is forced through the gill filaments, which, in turn, take oxygen from it.

Thirty-seven species of rockfish, so named because they hide from predators in rock caves, call the rainforest coast home too. There are brown rockfish, copper rockfish, widow rockfish (named for its jet-black color), yellowtail rockfish, chili pepper rockfish, quillback rockfish, black rockfish, vermilion rockfish and China rockfish, to name only a few. Harbor seals, sea lions and lingcod all eat rockfish, and many people consider them a delicacy. Rockfish are highly territorial. They claim and defend little rocky outcroppings deep in the ocean and can live more than a hundred years. Consequently, when too many are caught from a particular spot, it takes a long time for them to repopulate that area.

We often don't appreciate the importance of fish until they're lying on their sides and staring at us from a plate—next to a lemon wedge and a sprig of parsley. But to an ecosystem as vast and complex and ultimately fragile as the Great Bear Sea and Rainforest, fish, like plankton, are of limitless significance. There literally would be no Great Bear Rainforest without them.

FAR RIGHT: This black bear is able to expertly catch a salmon as it tries to migrate up a waterfall in one of the many salmon-spawning rivers found on the BC coast.

RIGHT: Tufted puffins may look like Amazonian parrots, but they live in the cold northern waters of the Great Bear Sea.

CHAPTER THREE
King Salmon

The Great Bear Rainforest and Sea abound with remarkable creatures, but if you were asked to name the most remarkable creature of all, what would it be? The spirit bear? The grizzly? The wolf? It may surprise you to know that most people who live in the rainforest would choose the salmon. That's right, the fish.

The Pacific salmon is one of the most extraordinary animals in the rainforest because without it—all five species of it—the rainforest would be a very different place. And if that isn't wondrous, what is?

To appreciate how miraculous salmon are, consider first their amazing ability to live the first and last parts of their lives in fresh water and the years in between at sea. That represents a colossal physiological change, not unlike the tadpole's remarkable

LEFT: **A school of pink salmon swims upstream in hopes of giving birth to a new generation of fish. Pinks are the most abundant of the five species of salmon in the Great Bear Sea.**

MARITIME MORSELS

How do First Nations honor the salmon?

Aboriginal people celebrate the salmon with ceremonies that show respect for a species that not only sustains their families with nourishment but is also integral to their culture and history. Some First Nations return the first salmon that is caught back to the sea as a gesture of respect. Others will hold on to the fish and make it the focus of a number of different rituals. The carcass may be placed on an altar, blessed, and then pointed upriver to show its spirit the way home. Sometimes only certain people will be allowed to eat it. When it's cleaned, its bones may be buried or, in some cases, returned to the river so it can reconstitute itself and continue its journey. Salmon are also featured in First Nations art. Curved like a crescent moon, they often take a proud place alongside figures of bears, eagles, wolves and whales on totem poles and in decorations on longhouses and other important buildings.

transformation into a frog. Except the salmon manages this change not once, but twice: first when a salmon fry leaves its river of birth and enters the sea to become a smolt, and then years later when the fully grown salmon returns to precisely the same river to fight its way upstream, spawn and die. Amazing.

All five species of Pacific salmon found in BC waters—chinook (also known as king), coho (silver), chum (dog), pink (humpback) and sockeye—begin life as embryos, developing in eggs laid by their mothers and fertilized by their fathers. But unlike the offspring of most mammals, including the rainforest's bears and wolves, young salmon never meet their parents. They never even see them because once fertilized eggs are safely covered by gravel and small rocks in a streambed, their parents die. This happens in the fall, and it isn't until late in the winter, or even the following spring, that newly hatched alevin emerge to begin their life's journey. Alevin live off a yolk sac attached to their sides for up to four months. Then they abandon it and swim out of the streambed as fry to search for prey. Some, like pinks and chum, head toward the ocean almost immediately, while others, like coho and sockeye, linger in the stream another year or even two.

However, most eggs never hatch. As many as eight out of every ten laid by a female salmon will be destroyed in one way or another before hatching. Some will become exposed to the elements and freeze over winter. Others will be washed away in a flood or dried up in a drought. Still others will be gobbled up by mink, otters, raccoons, ducks, gulls, bears, leeches or other fish. Trout, char and older salmon eat

both salmon eggs and newly hatched salmon fry. And if predators don't get these tiny fish, other dangers might. If it rains too much, weak swimmers won't be able to withstand the overflowing streams. If it rains too little, they may be isolated in pools where there isn't enough oxygen. All told, fewer than three in every ten salmon fry will survive long enough to reach the sea.

If they do succeed, the first place they'll get to is an estuary. These are at the edge of the rainforest where rivers meet the sea. Actually, they're where rivers merge with the sea, as it's impossible to say where one begins and the other ends. As fresh water flows into salt, so do millions of young salmon about to embark on the next grueling stage of their lives. For it's in these estuaries that salmon undergo that amazing transformation from a fresh-water to a salt-water fish. They also cease being fry and become what are called smolts.

TOP: **Fall is probably a bear's favorite time of year, because that's when salmon return to the forest to spawn. And there's nothing a rainforest grizzly bear appears to enjoy more than fishing.**

Estuaries are very productive pieces of nature. They're places where many different kinds of life flourish. The reason is that they're so full of nutrients. When a river empties into the sea, it brings more than just water and fish; it also brings organic matter collected en route from its source. And these nutrients feed the many species in an estuary, everything from plankton and insects to fish, birds and even whales.

With so much food available in estuaries, young smolts use the time they spend in them—days or months depending on the species—to adapt to salt water and to grow…and grow and grow. They may double or even triple in weight. But there is a trade-off. By spending so much time in one place, the smolts become easy pickings for predators like gulls, terns, kingfishers and herons. Larger fish, including bigger salmon, eat them too. Mature coho prey on pink and chum smolts. So to protect themselves, smolts start to school—that is, move about in large groups. Individual fish are still caught in schools, but not as many, because there's strength in numbers. Fish alert other fish to danger, and when they encircle each other, they protect each other from attack. This is a strategy salmon will use for the rest of their lives, particularly as they move into the ocean.

A salmon's life at sea is the part of its life cycle that represents the greatest unknown to us. Salmon can spend up to four years in the open ocean, but what do they do there? How do they live? Where do they live? What do they eat? It's hard for us to know because it's almost impossible to track a salmon once it's in such

MARITIME MORSELS

Do spawning salmon always return to the river or streambeds where they were born?

Almost always, unless humans or nature have made a stream or river impassable for some reason. Then salmon will look for an alternative. The best example of this was when Mount St. Helens, a volcano in northern Washington State, erupted in 1980. Ash poured into the neighboring Toutle River and blocked it. So that year, salmon born in the Toutle River spawned in the nearby Kalama River instead.

LEFT: **Ancient fish traps like these were maintained for thousands of years by coastal First Nations. They are still common at the mouths of salmon-producing rivers.**

a vast theater. When it comes to northeast Pacific salmon, scientists do know that when smolts leave their estuaries, they follow currents north to Alaska, then turn east toward Russia and south to the open ocean. That's a journey of thousands of kilometers. And they know that salmon continue to feed. Sand lance, herring, smaller salmon, crabs and squid are all staples of a salmon's diet. And of course, they are also fed upon. Seals, sea lions, dolphins and orcas eat them. As do halibut, lamprey eels and salmon sharks. Humans too. We eat vast quantities of them, which is why if a salmon is ever seen in the open sea, it's usually on the end of a line or in a net.

Nevertheless, millions do survive long enough to begin the greatest mystery of all: how they find their home rivers when it's time to spawn and die.

BOTTOM: **When you're a fish, the Great Bear Sea can be one dangerous place thanks to all the creatures—like this river otter—who are out to catch you.**

TOP: **How a spawning salmon, like this chum, manages to return to its home streambed in the fall is one of nature's greatest mysteries.**

Some scientists suggest that each river has its own distinct smell. Or maybe there's some kind of electrical current in the ocean that shows the salmon the right way. Perhaps it has to do with the position of the sun at a particular time of day. Maybe salmon have a built-in compass that we can neither see nor understand. Maybe it's a combination of all these things.

Tlingit and Haida First Nations say the salmon represent a race of spirits who live in human form beneath the sea. Then once a year at the beginning of fall, those spirits assume the bodies of salmon and swim upstream to feed the Native people on land. This is as good an explanation as any because the fact is that we simply don't know.

Nevertheless it's at this point when salmon begin their most momentous journey of all—swimming upriver to their birthplace to reproduce, die and,

in so doing, feed the rainforest. And this journey is made all the more demanding because they will not feed again once they start swimming upriver. Instead, they'll use every ounce of strength they've accumulated in fat and muscle to get where they have to go.

Pacific salmon can travel up to twelve days with no rest. They will encounter rushing white water, leap through waterfalls and over large rocks, and confront countless other obstacles. And during this final journey, the salmon undergo one more transformation. Put crudely, they turn ugly. Those handsome silvery torpedoes turn flabby. Their fins fray and tear. The female's stomachs swell, and their gums recede. Males develop a nasty-looking upper jaw and a deformed humpback, like the famous French hero

MARITIME MORSELS

How does a salmon swim?
Using a side-to-side motion driven by its tail and the rear half of its body. It uses its pectoral fins (the ones on its chest) for steering, and its ventral and dorsal fins (the fins on its stomach and back) to stay upright. When salmon leap over rocks and into waterfalls, they do it by employing a fierce whipping motion in their tails. In the middle of a leap, a salmon can "fly" as fast as 21 kilometers, or 14 miles, an hour.

FAR LEFT: **The race to reach the spawning ground is one of the most dramatic in the Great Bear Rainforest and all of nature.**

LEFT: **Coastal wolves rely on salmon as one of their principle food staples. You may not associate wolves with fishing, but in the Great Bear Rainforest, they do it all the time.**

MARITIME MORSELS

How far do salmon travel?

Given that no one has ever managed to follow a salmon from birth to death, it's hard to say with any real precision how far they travel at sea. But according to the Vancouver Aquarium, chinook salmon will traverse up to 16,000 kilometers (10,000 miles) through their North Pacific feeding grounds. That's four times the driving distance between Vancouver and Toronto or Los Angeles and New York. They also can travel more than 3,000 kilometers (1,800 miles) upstream when they spawn. On average they travel about 50 kilometers (30 miles) a day against the flow. Think what amazing athletes that makes them.

RIGHT: **When sockeye salmon reach their spawning grounds, they lose their silvery color and turn a bright shade of red. It's thought that this signals the male's readiness to breed.**

of *The Hunchback of Notre Dame*. Scientists think this hump helps males compete for a female, or it may make them easier targets for predators and take the attention off the females. When it comes to a mating pair, the female is always more important because she's the one with the eggs.

Males also change color from silver to a dull shade of green, purple or, in the case of sockeye, fire-engine red. Scientists don't know why, but it's thought that this change signals the male's readiness to breed. Females also change color to a duller green or red, perhaps for the same reason.

And if that weren't enough, it's at this stage of a salmon's life that hungry bears and wolves go fishing. They will feast on salmon for months. Some island wolves feed on them for a full four months of the year, while bears depend on them to supply most of the body fat that will see them through winter. And when you're as big as a bear, that could mean more than twenty-two kilograms (fifty pounds) of salmon in a single day. That's one big haul of fish!

Yet despite these dangers, some lucky salmon will manage to make it all the way back to their home beds to mate, lay eggs and die. Then their journey is complete.

Certainly by the time a salmon reaches its life's goal—that streamed from whence it came—it's a tired, battered shell of its former self. A boxer after a brutal fight. But they're still champions, because they're the ones who get to pass on their genes to future generations. At its most basic, that is what life is all about.

MARITIME MORSELS

How do salmon sense the world around them?

As far as scientists can tell, salmon see all the colors that we do as well as those of ultraviolet light, which we can't see. This suggests that when salmon look into the sea, they see something very different from what we do. The largest part of the salmon's brain, which is about the size of a peanut, is devoted to smelling, because it could be the scent of a particular river that draws the salmon back to spawn. The fact that salmon have such a sensitive sense of smell makes them particularly vulnerable to pollution, which may be one of many reasons why salmon stocks near cities are especially endangered.

Yet even after death, salmon go on giving life. When they're broken down into tiny pieces by the creatures who feed on them, they nourish the rainforest soil and ultimately its great trees. Researchers at the University of Victoria have determined that decomposing salmon provide the rainforest with thousands of pounds of life-giving fertilizer in each and every acre.

Thus the most wondrous creature in the rainforest isn't the grizzly or the wolf or the orca. It's the salmon. That silver flash of a fish that fishermen prize so highly and bears eat so hungrily. That piece of pink flesh we throw on a grill so casually each summer. What would the rainforest be without them?

RIGHT: **The millions of spawned-out salmon carcasses help fertilize trees and plants along the banks of the spawning rivers. So even in death salmon continue to benefit the rainforest ecosystem.**

FAR RIGHT: **It's the rare salmon that manages to make it all the way to its spawning ground. Most, like this coho, fall victim to any one of a dozen different dangers along the way.**

CHAPTER FOUR

On the Edge

W hen you stand at the ocean's edge, you can be sure that whatever you're looking at will change. Sometimes the sea is as quiet and playful as a young rainforest deer. Other times, it's like an angry old grizzly. At times like this it's best to stay out of its way. Waves crash like thunder, trees topple, branches break, and the wind whistles and howls. Waves over 30 meters (100 feet) tall and winds over 200 kilometers (125 miles) an hour have been recorded along the Great Bear Sea.

Life at sea really is that changeable, and for creatures that live at the sea's edge—the *intertidal zone*—those changes can occur in a single day. This chapter is about those creatures.

Even if you haven't heard the word before, you can probably figure out what the intertidal zone is

LEFT: **The stretch of beach between the high- and low-tide points is called the intertidal zone, and it is a place of immense natural beauty and productivity.**

if you've ever stood on a seashore. You'll know there's a point on that shore where the tide doesn't rise any higher or fall any lower. So when the tide is out, it's as if a wide wet stripe has been painted between those points. This stretch of beach or rocky shore is called the intertidal zone—the zone between the high- and low-tide marks. It takes a special kind of creature to live in this zone because the living conditions are so harsh. One minute you're submerged under a few meters of cold water, and the next you're high and dry under a warm sun. It's not every creature that can withstand such drastic change twice a day every day. Yet hundreds do. Barnacles, mussels, seaweed, clams, abalone, whelks and chitons (pronounced *ky-tons*) are among the most abundant of all creatures in the Great Bear Sea—and on the planet. They're also some

BOTTOM: **Seaweed covered in a fresh layer of herring eggs, found along found along the intertidal zone have to be extremely tough given that they live part of their lives exposed to the sun and part submerged under cold water.**

of the easiest wild creatures for people to spot and study, because when the tide goes out, they're there for anyone to see.

But the intertidal zone is more than just a strip of wet earth. It's also a meeting place where a variety of animals that live on land, in the air and even farther out at sea all come together. The bears who give the Great Bear Rainforest its name lumber along the intertidal zone scavenging for food. You wouldn't think a barnacle, clam or crab would make much of a meal for a grizzly, but if they work all day digging for them, it can amount to a lot of food. River otters spend most of their time on land, but they get their food from the ocean. The intertidal zone is like a buffet table for them.

Small brown mink live in burrows under cedar and spruce trees, and hide from predators in them.

TOP: **This black bear eats recently laid herring eggs that have attached themselves to the rocky shore. Herring spawn in the spring, making their eggs the first real treat newly awakened bears have to enjoy after a long winter's sleep.**

MARITIME MORSELS

How long can a clam live?

In 1982 an Atlantic clam was found to have 220 annual growth rings in its shell, meaning it was 220 years old! The longest-living clam on the Pacific coast is thought to be the geoduck, a long-necked creature that doesn't look very much like a clam. Geoducks can live up to 140 years. Other clams can live about 20 years—that is, if birds, sea otters and clam diggers don't dig them up first.

RIGHT: **Sea stars, mussels and barnacles cling to rocks as waves smash in upon them from the open Pacific.**

But at night, they and their cousins, the raccoons, take to the rainforest shoreline to feast on mussels and other intertidal delicacies. Even deer and mountain goats eat seaweed in winter. None of these creatures lives in the intertidal zone, but they all depend on it in some way for their survival. Does that make them marine creatures too? It's a puzzling question to answer.

For creatures who do live their whole lives in the intertidal zone, the extremes they can endure—like how much sun they can withstand and for how long—determine where in the zone they live. That's why, when the tide is out, you will see distinct layers of creatures, each one farther from the high-tide line than its neighbor. It's like a many-layered cake with each layer representing a different zone of life.

The Great Bear Rainforest shoreline is long and varied. There are sandy beaches, mud flats and estuaries where eel grass—a kind of underwater grass—grows and blooms. But much of the forest shore is rocky, rugged and remote, which is ideal habitat for intertidal creatures.

Many people find it hard to think of barnacles as living things. When they're crushed together on the surface of a rock in an ugly, knobbly (and really painful if you walk on them with bare feet) carpet, they look like stucco on the side of a house. But barnacles *are* living creatures. It's just that when the tide goes out, the creatures inside those tooth-like shells stop moving. This is also true of mollusks like oysters, mussels and clams. We know there's a fleshy, tasty creature inside each of the oyster and mussel shells that decorate Pacific shorelines like

MARITIME MORSELS

How nutritious is seaweed?

Very. Seaweed is full of calcium—even more than broccoli has—and it contains as much protein as beans and nuts. It's also a great source of fiber, which is important for your digestion. No wonder some supermarkets now sell dried seaweed on their shelves. It's one more good reason to eat your greens!

RIGHT: **This grizzly mother and her cub dig under rocks to find salmon eggs buried deep in the gravel. Turning over boulders is hard work for a human, but it's child's play to a grizzly.**

FAR RIGHT: **In addition to being places of enormous richness and productivity, intertidal zones are places of outstanding natural beauty. Sea stars come in a variety of colors, but purple and red are the most common.**

plates on a sideboard. But when the tide's out, who'd know, because all their shells have clammed up.

Bears would. In the Great Bear Rainforest, black bears, grizzlies and spirit bears alike comb the shore for clams, oysters, mussels and barnacles. Some bears break the shells off the rocks and suck out the fleshy creatures inside. Others eat everything, including the shell. If you're a human being, that's hard work. Pulling a barnacle shell off a rock is almost impossible. It's as if they've been Crazy-glued on. But if you're a bear, other than being hard on your teeth, it's no sweat. Many seabirds find ways to open shellfish too. Gulls, cormorants, oystercatchers, herons, ducks and other shorebirds either pry them open with their bills or pull them loose, fly high over the beach with

the hapless clam or mussel in their mouth and then drop it on the rocks below. When the shell smashes, the creature inside is a quick swallow away.

There are hundreds of different kinds of shellfish living within the intertidal zones of the Great Bear Rainforest, but they all conform to one of four basic shell types. The first are *bivalves*. These are creatures protected by two shells joined by a hinge. Think of a clam, an oyster or a mussel. They all have two shells that fold together like hands folded in prayer. There are about seventy species of bivalves living within the northeast Pacific intertidal zone. Then there are *gastropods*. These are shellfish protected by a single whorled shell. Think of the way a soft ice-cream cone builds to a swirled point. That's whorled. Abalone, snails and whelks all have whorled shells. Next are *tuskshells*,

BOTTOM: **Bat stars and red sea urchins like these are common in areas of strong tidal current.**

which are creatures with shells shaped like—guess what?—an elephant or walrus tusk, only smaller. Finally there are *chitons*, which are shellfish with shells made of overlapping plates like little shields, or shingles on a really tiny roof.

Another intertidal zone resident is the purple shore crab, named for its color (although it can also be reddish brown or greenish yellow). Purple shore crabs are common along northeastern Pacific shores and can often be seen running helter-skelter for dear life. Look under almost any rock and you're bound to find one—along with many other crab and shrimp species. Rocks provide crabs with hiding places, and if those hiding places are removed, the crabs become vulnerable to predators. Is it any wonder they panic?

Among those predators is the largest and arguably the most impressive intertidal resident of all: the sea star. The sunflower star, for example, is the largest of its kind in the world. It can grow to a meter (three feet) wide and boast as many as twenty-four legs. Many different species of such multi-legged and colorful stars occupy the shoreline of the Great Bear Rainforest, including the ocher sea star, named for its orangey brown color. But here's a funny thing. Most ocher sea stars are purple. A rich, deep, royal purple. This only happens when the ocher sea star lives on a beach protected from the open sea by a body of land. Why are some ocher sea stars orange and others purple? Nobody knows. It's another of nature's intriguing mysteries.

Sea stars are voracious. A single ocher sea star can eat eighty big California mussels a year, so if there

MARITIME MORSELS

Why should we call sea stars sea stars, not starfish?

Because sea stars aren't fish. They don't have gills, scales or fins like most fish, and they move differently too. Whereas fish use their tails to propel themselves through the water, sea stars walk on their tiny tube-like feet. We call them stars because most have five legs or points like a star. But many have more. And if they lose a point, they can grow it back. It takes a while—up to a year—but if the sea star is left alone and not hurt again, it'll be good as new. Eventually.

are a lot of ocher sea stars around, they'll have a big impact on mussel populations. Consequently we find that mussel colonies often move out of their reach. If you study the intertidal zone, you'll notice that many mussels attach themselves to rocks at a point too high for sea stars. Clever mussels. So near yet so far.

Mud flats are just that—stretches of mud lying dark gray and dormant under the rainforest sky. That is, until the tide moves in. Then they come to life thanks to all the simple organisms that live in the flats but move only underwater. When they do, birds swoop in to feed on them. In spring and summer thousands of shorebirds like sand pipers and plovers descend on mud flats to feast on the annual harvest of shrimp and worms that flows in with the tide.

MARITIME MORSELS

Where does a crab hide its teeth?
Believe it or not, in its stomach. Not only that, but crabs can swim. Crabs have swim paddles on their legs that help them get from one place to another. And like a lizard that loses its tail, if a crab loses its claw, in time the claw will grow back.

FAR LEFT: **Black turnstones, one of the many species of shorebirds found along the coast of the Great Bear Sea, take wing over a calm stretch of water.**

LEFT: **A spotted sand piper uses its long pointy bill to search for food along the shore of the Great Bear Sea.**

MARITIME MORSELS

How many different kinds of shell shapes do mollusks have?

Each mollusk's shell is as individual as the mollusk wearing it. They can be round, oval, elongated, wing-shaped, worm-like, flat and compressed, or globular. In bivalves, both halves of the shell are usually the same size and shape, but not always. Some scallop and oyster species have shells where one half is bigger than the other. Presumably that doesn't bother the scallop or oyster, but imagine if one of your hands or feet was bigger than the other. You might feel a little lopsided.

In fact, about twenty different species of shorebirds use mud flats at one time or another, making them a much livelier place than their unappealing name suggests.

For people, the best thing about intertidal zones is that they're like natural aquariums. When the tide goes out, some water remains trapped in pools, and these so-called tidal pools provide a great opportunity to watch and learn. But attractive as tide pools are, life is tough for the creatures in them because temperature differences can be so extreme. Most marine animals require fairly stable temperatures to survive. This is why most intertidal lifeforms hide under rocks or squeeze into cracks between them when the tide goes out. Only a special kind of organism can survive in a tide pool.

One such group of organisms is the anemones, which resemble colorful flowers blooming underwater. Except, instead of waving in the breeze, their "petals"—actually their tentacles (they *are* carnivorous predators)—float in the eddies. When a single anemone gets big, it splits in two. That way a tide pool can fill up with near identical anemones in no time. Then the pool becomes a sea garden.

Estuaries are where salt marshes develop. Like mud flats, they are tremendously productive. Estuary plants must be able to tolerate both fresh and salt water. The most widespread of them is Lyngby's sedge, a plant with long blade-like leaves that feed everything from grizzlies to deer to geese. Lyngby's sedge grows so densely at the rainforest edge that it's as if nature planted fields of it. Sometimes in a really rich pocket of soil, sedge can grow over two and a half

meters (eight feet) tall—tall enough to hide bears, wolves and even people. Many shorebirds, including ducks, geese and wild swans, gather in estuaries to feed on the rich plant and animal life in them. And they don't waste a thing. They strip seeds from the marsh plants, gobble up the seaweed and pull roots from the estuary floor.

Finally, there are undersea rainforests. Really. When there's enough light at the sea's surface to allow photo-synthesis, and enough nutrients to allow biological growth, a seaweed called *kelp* grows so densely that it forms actual forests. There are more than 600 species of seaweed on the British Columbia coast, but bull kelp is the most impressive. Bull kelp anchor themselves to the rocky sea floor and will grow as much as 0.6 meters (2 feet) in a single day. The biggest bull kelp can be 30 meters (100 feet) tall, providing food and shelter for

TOP: **Sea anemones may look like flowers, but they're animals. And what look like petals waving in the breeze are tentacles floating in the current.**

many marine organisms. Eagles use dry kelp to build nests, and First Nations people used to weave kelp into fishing lines to catch halibut.

When people look at a kelp bed or forest, what they see from the surface is the kelp's thin stipes (stems), their round balloon-like floats that attach to the stipes and float like buoys, and their long brown fronds, or leaves. What people can't see is how much life teems in kelp forests below that surface. Schools of perch, herring and rockfish dart among their fronds. Crabs scurry at their base. And in places where sea otters have been reintroduced, furry brown tails flash back and forth. Sea otters love kelp forests. They make beds out of the fronds. Sea urchins love them too, but for a different reason. They eat them. But thanks to sea otters, who eat urchins, a balance is struck. However, sea otters are still absent from most of the Great Bear Sea because so many were slaughtered during the eighteenth, nineteenth and early twentieth centuries (more about this in Chapter Five). Consequently, that balance has been tipped. Urchins have been allowed to feast unfettered on kelp, all but destroying the once endless beds. This has also affected rockfish because they no longer have hiding places. As a result, their numbers have declined too.

Now, thanks to the reintroduction of sea otters to parts of the West Coast, the situation is righting itself. The otters eat the sea urchins, which can no longer devour the kelp. But it will take patience and time for the historical balance to reassert itself. It goes to show—again—just how fragile nature is.

RIGHT: **Color, texture, movement and life. They are the hallmarks of any intertidal zone, including those in the Great Bear Sea.**

CHAPTER FIVE
Clowns of the Kelp Beds

"Cute" is not a scientific term. Ask any scientist, and he or she will tell you that just because an animal is cute, it isn't any better or more deserving of protection than an animal that isn't. Even so, when it comes to the Great Bear Sea, cute doesn't come any cuter than sea otters. With their round heads, marble eyes, large noses and long absentminded-professor whiskers, they're as cute as cute gets in the marine world. A video of two of them holding each other's paws in the Vancouver Aquarium has attracted more than eighteen million hits on YouTube. (Google "Otters holding hands" and see for yourself.) Now *that's* cute.

So even though scientists are correct when they say cuteness isn't a barometer of worth, the fact that sea otters are as cute as they are may be a good thing because they still need all the help they can get.

LEFT: **A hundred years ago, hunting all but eliminated the fuzzy face of the sea otter from the Great Bear Sea. Today, happily, small populations are returning to their native waters.**

Between the 1700s and the early 1900s, the demand for their luxuriant fur almost wiped them out. Today, that same cuddly fur may be what saves them.

Before European and Asian hunters began slaughtering them, Pacific sea otters numbered more than a million individuals off the coasts of Japan, Russia, Alaska, British Columbia and the US mainland. But because of that hunt, they all but vanished a hundred years ago. In fact, the only reason people decided to stop hunting them was that they thought there were none left to hunt. Nevertheless, in 1911 the governments of Russia, Japan, the United States and Great Britain (which represented Canada at the time) signed an international agreement calling for an immediate and permanent end to hunting—just in case a few had managed to escape.

BOTTOM: **Once there were more than a million sea otters in the North Pacific, but demand for their amazingly dense pelts almost wiped them out. Today they number in the low thousands.**

PHOTOGRAPH BY BRAD HILL

Happily, some had. Fewer than two thousand, people think, scattered in a handful of remote bays and islands off the coasts of Japan, Alaska and California. But none (at least none we know of) in the Great Bear Sea. So if they were ever going to be seen bobbing, weaving and diving off the central British Columbia coast again, they were going to have to be brought there. Which is what happened between 1969 and 1972 when eighty-nine sea otters were transported from their home in Alaska to the northwest coast of Vancouver Island, the southern-most tip of the Great Bear Rainforest.

Today, thanks to that reintroduction, about 2,500 sea otters live there, in addition to about 500 or so near the Heiltsuk village of Bella Bella across Hecate Strait from the southernmost tip of Haida Gwaii. And the good news is that they're expanding their range each year.

TOP: **Sea otters rarely leave the safety of the ocean, but occasionally they can be seen hauled out like seals on rocky islets.**

MARITIME MORSELS

Are sea otters related to river otters?

Yes. They're both members of the weasel family, which also includes skunks, minks, sables, ermines, wolverines, badgers and—guess what?—weasels. But river otters look and behave differently from sea otters. Their legs are longer, so getting around on land is easy for them. Their tails are longer too. And while river otters can spend time in either fresh or sea water, sea otters must live in the ocean.

Sea otters are marine mammals, meaning that even though they spend all their time in water (and very rarely touch land), they take oxygen from air, not water. That's why they spend most of their time at or near the ocean's surface. Even their dives aren't very deep. The average sea otter dive is about thirty-three feet deep and no more than a minute long—just long enough to grab something tasty off an undersea rock or dig up a clam in a shallow sea basin and bring it to the surface. Because that's where otters feed. When an otter goes fishing—or clam digging—he or she will bring his urchin or clam to the surface and eat it there.

Sometimes otters grab more than just one clam or crab at a time. They have special pouches under their forelegs in which they can carry shellfish or other food—squid, octopus or fish—while they continue foraging for something else. The pouch acts as a kind of handbag. If they don't carry food in it, they may carry a stone. Then when they catch a shellfish or a fish, they'll use the stone to crack open the shell or kill the fish. It's a tool. Once upon a time biologists thought only humans used tools. Now we know that many non-human animals use them too, including sea otters.

Another big challenge sea otters face is staying warm. Don't forget, it's cold in the north Pacific—the average temperature is about 7 degrees Celsius (45 degrees Fahrenheit), far too cold for a human to go swimming without a wetsuit. One way sea otters stay warm is to move constantly and maintain a high *metabolic rate*. This is a term used to describe the amount of energy an animal expends in a certain length of time.

You know if you get cold that you can exert yourself to get warm. Get your blood flowing by doing some jumping jacks or running on the spot. Sea otters are the same. But movement requires energy, and energy requires food—lots of it. Otters have to eat the equivalent of one-quarter of their body weight each day. This means they have to fish day and night, and explains why they have to take frequent naps. They sleep on their backs—sometimes in a kelp bed—with their forepaws folded under their chins or over their eyes. And yes, that does give new meaning to the word *cute*.

Then there are their coats—those glossy fur coats that were formerly prized so highly and exploited so mercilessly. The otter's coat is something to behold. The thickest sea otter coat contains up to one million hairs per square inch! That's mind-boggling if you consider that the average German shepherd coat contains a

TOP: **A sea otter's coat has up to a million hairs per square inch. That makes it phenomenally dense and thick. It also allows sea otters to float on the surface and stay warm in what is usually a very cold sea.**

MARITIME MORSELS

Why are oil spills so devastating to sea otters?

When oil seeps into a sea otter's fur, that fur loses its buoyancy and its ability to insulate the otter. That, in turn, can lead to pneumonia or hypothermia (a condition in which the animal's temperature drops below the point where normal metabolism can take place). What's more, when sea otters try to groom fur that's been soaked in oil, they ingest the oil into their lungs, which causes severe damage to the lungs as well as their kidneys and liver.

RIGHT: **When sea otter pups are three months old, they dive by themselves for the first time. But unlike you, they never have to be taught to swim. They just know how.**

PHOTOGRAPH BY BRAD HILL

mere 40,000 hairs per square inch. Or that the average human head—that's the entire head, not just a square inch of it—has a measly 100,000. But maintaining a coat that thick and lustrous requires effort. Consequently, sea otters spend a lot of time grooming themselves and, if they're parents, grooming their young.

But their real secret to keeping warm is to surround the hairs in those amazingly dense coats with layers of tiny air bubbles. All other marine mammals—the seals, sea lions and whales you'll meet in future chapters—have thick layers of blubber to keep them warm. Not sea otters. All that lies between their skin and the cold, dark deep is their fur and a layer of air bubbles, which is trapped in that fur. That's why it's so important for sea otters to keep their coats in such good condition. A matted coat wouldn't allow air to pass between their hairs, and that could mean the otter freezing to death. Cloaking themselves in air bubbles (imagine a kind of free-forming bubble wrap) also makes floating easier, but diving more difficult. It's the price sea otters pay to stay warm—and one of the main reasons they fish in shallow water.

For reasons scientists don't understand, some otter mothers have pups on land, while others have them at sea. But whatever the reason, once they've had one—and they never have more than one at a time—moms from both camps will dedicate the next six months to teaching that pup about life on the waves.

Like most mammal mothers, sea otters are fiercely protective of their offspring. When pups are very young, otter moms carry them around all the time. So if a bald eagle starts circling overhead in a menacing way

(eagles, sharks and killer whales are a few of the sea otter's natural enemies), a sea otter mom and her pup will disappear in no time. If the pup is really small, Mom will tuck him or her under a foreleg and then dive to a safe depth with the pup nestled under her shoulder. If the pup's too big, she'll grab him or her with her teeth and pull the pup under that way.

Otter pups have to be at least three months old before they can dive by themselves, though they float like corks from the day they're born. There are times, however, when sea otter moms have no choice but to leave pups alone. When they dive for food, for example, a pup would only get in the way. One of the best and safest places a mom can leave her pup is in a kelp forest. And because they know there's safety in numbers, it isn't unusual to see sea otters floating

BOTTOM: **Like people, sea otters are very social. It isn't unusual to see them floating and diving in groups of ten, twenty or even a hundred animals.**

PHOTOGRAPH BY ROY TOFT/
NATIONAL GEOGRAPHIC STOCK

and diving in large groups of ten, twenty or even a hundred—at least in places where otter populations are large enough to make such groups (called rafts) possible. Imagine how big these rafts might have been in the days before the fur hunters arrived. They would have looked like otter islands.

Even today sea otters remain in danger because of pollution, overfishing and climate change. But at least we recognize that they aren't limitless, and that if we work hard and carefully to protect them, they'll survive.

Of course, being cute doesn't hurt them either.

TOP: **Sea otters—and cross jellyfish—are often found hidden in thick floating kelp forests like this one. Kelp also provide sea urchins, the sea otter's favorite food source, with food of their own.**

CHAPTER SIX

Fins and Flippers

Today people love seals and sea lions. "Look, a seal," we say with real joy if we see one frolicking in the waves. If a pup is left alone on a rock, we worry. We want to make sure it's all right.

What a difference forty years makes. It was only in the 1970s that harbor seals, the most familiar and arguably most endearing of northeast Pacific seals, finally won a government reprieve from being shot on sight. Until then, commercial fishermen blamed them for biting into their catch, so from 1913 to 1964, Canada's Department of Fisheries and Oceans rewarded anyone who killed a harbor seal with cash—a bounty. Not surprisingly, harbor seal numbers crashed, and it was only when hunting officially ended ten years later that they were able to recover.

LEFT: **Sea lions, like these photogenic females, are always curious when a scuba diver visits their territory. Seals and sea lions are known as pinnipeds, from the Latin roots *pinna*, meaning "wing" or "fin," and *ped*, meaning "foot." Thus, seals and sea lions are said to be fin- or feather-footed creatures.**

Other marine species suffered too. The northern fur seal, the Steller sea lion and the northern elephant seal, all inhabitants of the Great Bear Sea, were hunted almost to extinction for their fur and their blubber (which was used in oil lamps) in the nineteenth and twentieth centuries. *Conservation* simply wasn't a word that was used back then. People took what they needed without worrying about what those needs cost.

Happily, that's no longer true for the seals and sea lions of the Great Bear Sea. Yes, they continue to face that same litany of twenty-first-century calamities—overfishing, pollution, climate change, wayward driftnets and industrial shipping among them—but they are safe from organized slaughter. Consequently, like the sea otter, they've come back. The Great Bear Sea is once again becoming a friendly, welcoming

BOTTOM: **This adorable face belongs to an elephant seal pup. When he grows up, he could weigh as much as 2,000 kilograms or 4,400 pounds. Chances are he won't be quite so cute then.**

place for species that just a short time ago were rarely, if ever, seen.

All seals and sea lions are what biologists call *pinnipeds*, a word derived from two Latin roots: *pinna*, meaning "wing" or "fin," and *ped*, meaning "foot." So pinnipeds are said to be "fin-footed" or "feather-footed" creatures. Except, instead of feet they have fins—two near their chests and two at their backs, like the flippers you might wear when you swim.

And even though seals and sea lions differ in size, color, and where and how they live, they're all basically the same shape. They all have rounded or slightly flattened faces, small ears and slit-like nostrils that close up tight when they're underwater. They also have streamlined bodies that look like sacks of blubber on land, but move like mermaids in water. They differ greatly in size, however. The average harbor seal weighs thirty-five kilograms (seventy-seven pounds) while the biggest elephant seal weighs sixty times that much.

Pinnipeds also have fur. But it's not just to keep them warm. It's also there to protect their bodies when they rest on or move over barnacles, mussels and sharp rocks. What really keeps seals and sea lions warm is a cushiony layer of *subcutaneous* ("under the skin") fat or blubber—the same blubber that made them targets for hunters. You'll know from your own experience that you feel the cold less when you wear a cushiony layer of thermal underwear in the winter. Non-human animals are the same. So when you live your life in a place as cold as the northeast Pacific, a thick layer of padding is essential. It also helps seals and sea lions stay afloat, and even provides them with

MARITIME MORSELS

What sounds do pinnipeds make?

Many seal and sea lion species get loud and proud during their mating seasons, and some of their vocal selections sound eerily like songs. Most, however, are honks, hoots, snorts, barks, roars, short sharp gulps and bagpipe wheezes. Seals certainly are capable of imitating sounds, particularly those of other seals. But what this ability does for them is something for seals to know and scientists to find out.

a temporary food supply if external food sources run short. In that way it's like a personal store of food—there to dip into if they must.

Seals and sea lions eat fish. They eat other sea creatures too—squid and octopus among them—but mainly fish. Those streamlined bodies enable them to chase fish easily, and their ability to hold their breath for a long time means they can stay underwater long enough to catch the fish they're chasing. They do this by slowing their heartbeats, a process that helps them conserve oxygen. Adult seals and sea lions can slow their heart rates from as many as 120 beats per minute to as few as four. This allows sea lions to remain underwater for an hour or longer. And in an hour your chances of finding a fish—or an octopus or squid—are much better than if you were

BOTTOM: **Harbor seals are common throughout the Great Bear Sea and much of the Pacific, but like a human fingerprint, no two are alike. They come in a variety of colors, from black to brown to gray to white, and some even sport spots like a leopard.**

only there for a minute. Not only that, they can dive very deep. Elephant seals can plunge more than 900 meters (3,000 feet) to search for hagfish, squid and other deep-water delicacies. That's more than the height of two Empire State Buildings.

So how do seals and sea lions differ? Wouldn't you know it, the distinction is anything but definitive because one of the Great Bear Rainforest's principal seal residents, the northern fur seal, is more of a sea lion than a seal. Yet biologists continue to call them seals. Go figure. Nevertheless, in general, seals and sea lions differ in four ways:

- Sea lions (and the northern fur seal) have external ear flaps; seals don't.
- Seals swim mainly with their hind flippers; sea lions (and the northern fur seal) swim mainly with their fore fins.

TOP: **Steller sea lions are as graceful as mermaids underwater, but on land they're more like slow-moving bulldozers.**

MARITIME MORSELS

How do pinnipeds swim?

All pinnipeds rely heavily on sinuous muscle movements in their bodies to propel themselves forward, but whereas sea lions depend mainly on their fore fins, seals rely on their hind flippers. When pinnipeds dive underwater, their pupils expand to a remarkable degree to help them see. They're also thought to hear well underwater and have an excellent sense of smell. Such a good sense of smell, in fact, that they can pick up the odors of potential predators several kilometers away.

RIGHT: **Some of the largest Steller sea lion rookeries (breeding places) in the north Pacific are found along the BC coast.**

- Seals can live in both fresh and salt water; sea lions (and the northern fur seal) can only live in the ocean.
- Sea lions can turn their hind flippers forward; seals can't.

Because the Great Bear Rainforest is so hard to get to, not everyone will have the chance to see its marvelous maritime residents. But if you live or visit anywhere along the coast of North America, chances are good that you will be able to see one of its favorite ambassadors, the harbor seal. Harbor seals are the most widely distributed pinnipeds in the world. Even big cities don't daunt them. Now that urban harbors aren't as polluted as they once were, you can see harbor seals in places like Vancouver, Seattle and San Francisco. Even New York.

At up to 1.6 meters (5 feet) in length and 80 kilograms (176 pounds) in weight, they're about the size and shape of a densely packed duffel bag. But a duffel bag packed with charm. With their cute faces and puppyish get-up-and-go, they are among the rainforest's most captivating residents.

Harbor seals live their whole lives close to shore. They also don't migrate the way other pinnipeds do. Once they choose a territory, they stick to it. And when it comes to diving, they're not ambitious. Harbor seal dives last for about three minutes, and they're seldom more than 100 meters (330 feet) deep.

They're also fairly solitary—except when it's time to breed. Then, like all pinnipeds, they converge on breeding sites up and down the coast where, for a month or so, males will stake territories and lay claim

to mates, and females will give birth. The farther south they are, the earlier the breeding season. Because the Great Bear Rainforest is so far north, breeding takes place when warmer weather comes, in July and August.

Like sea otters, pinnipeds usually give birth to one pup at a time. Harbor seal pups weigh about ten kilograms (twenty-two pounds) at birth and are able to crawl and swim within a few hours, without anyone having to show them how. They have to because life is dangerous. Seal pups are eaten by killer whales, sharks, wolves and large birds. Even sea otters have been known to drown harbor seal pups. Consequently, harbor seal moms are very protective, at least until their pups are weaned, at about four to six weeks old. Then they're on their own. Harbor seal dads, like so many of nature's fathers, have little to do with raising young.

Northern elephant seals, the largest pinnipeds in the rainforest and the second-largest seal in the world (only the southern elephant seal is bigger), are the harbor seals' polar opposites. Adult males, or bulls, can weigh as much as 2,000 kilograms, or 4,400 pounds, and grow to be 4 meters (about 13 feet) long. They also live most of their lives far from any shore, as much as 8,000 kilometers (5,000 miles) away. Practically another world. So if harbor seals are the homebodies of the rainforest's water world, northern elephant seals are its explorers. So much so that it's hard to regard them as residents at all. They don't even breed near the Great Bear Rainforest. Instead they go to California or Mexico, where it's warm.

Yet when breeding season is over, usually in early spring, northern elephant seals return to the northern

MARITIME MORSELS

How do you tell one harbor seal from another?

By its coat, which is short, thick and patterned. In fact, just like a human's fingerprints, each harbor seal has his or her own unique cut and shade of hair. Patterns range from white, silver or light gray coats with dark rings or spots to beige or brown coats with light or dark rings to dark gray or even black coats with light rings. If you live in a city by the sea, you may see harbor seals, as they are frequent visitors to city harbors—hence their name.

LEFT: **These gregarious and very loud sea lions can be found in groups of over a thousand clamorous individuals along portions of the north and central BC coast.**

Pacific waters that give them their name. (The "elephant" comes from the fact that when males are sexually mature, they develop long noses or *probosci* that somewhat resemble elephant trunks.) Although northern elephant seals are difficult to find, if you're sailing along gently or *put-putting* quietly in a motorboat, you may be lucky enough to spot one, or even a few, sitting upright in the open water, asleep, with nothing but the ocean to hold them up. How's that for a neat trick? It's easy to mistake them for deadheads (partially submerged logs).

For the most part, however, northern elephant seals spend hardly any time at the ocean's surface. They're too busy fishing and diving for squid, ratfish, some deep-water shark species, eels and other bottom-dwelling life. They'll make as many as three dives an

BOTTOM: **No circus seals here. These massive Steller sea lions take a rest on the windswept and rugged outer coast of the Great Bear Sea.**

hour, each lasting about twenty minutes. That barely leaves them time to catch their breath.

The northern fur seal—the seal with all the sea lion features—gets its name from its dense dark fur. Though not as dense as the sea otter's—it has about 57,000 hairs per square inch versus the otter's million—its fur is and was lustrous enough to tantalize those rapacious fur traders too. Several million fur seals were killed in fairly short order, and like the sea otter, the species almost disappeared. Remarkably, it wasn't until 1957 that hunting fur seals at sea was made illegal, and not until 1983 that killing them in breeding colonies, or rookeries, was outlawed. Today their population is thought to be just over a million, though thanks to those usual twenty-first-century crises—overfishing, pollution, climate change and driftnets—that number is dropping again.

Like elephant seals, northern fur seals spend a lot of time at sea. But they don't venture as far out. Mostly you can find them within 50 to 100 kilometers (30 to 60 miles) of the coast. They're also smaller than elephant seals. The largest are only 270 kilograms (600 pounds) or so, and about 2 meters (6 feet 6 inches) long. And they're easier to see. If it's daytime, you might find them asleep in the waves like an elephant seal. Except fur seals sleep on their sides. Night and early in the morning are when they fish, and they may spend as many as ten days at sea without ever going near land.

Northern fur seals usually travel in pairs, or occasionally in groups of three, but breeding time is party time. Because they're so particular about where they breed—on just four small islands off the coast

MARITIME MORSELS

How did marine mammals evolve?

It's thought that all marine mammals evolved from land animals. Those animals, whatever they were, probably moved into the sea to take advantage of new food resources and to avoid earthbound predators. When that happened, they evolved certain adaptations, such as fins, flippers and the ability to hold their breath for a long time.

MARITIME MORSELS

What should you do if you find a seal pup on its own?

Initially nothing. Occasionally a mother seal will abandon her young, but such abandonments are rare. So when you do see a seal pup on its own, the best thing to do is watch and wait and stay out of sight. That's because mother seals often leave their young onshore while they go fishing, and they may be gone for hours. But when they do return, if they see a strange two-legged creature hovering over their pup, they may decide to abandon it after all. If a pup really has been abandoned, report it to your nearest marine mammal rescue center.

of Alaska in the Bering Sea—breeding time means a melee of activity. With the entire northern fur seal population present, is it any wonder that from May to September these islands are as busy, noisy and crowded as four islands can be?

Steller sea lions were named after an eighteenth-century German botanist, zoologist and explorer named Georg Wilhelm Steller, who, in addition to discovering said sea lion and the Steller jay (a close cousin of the blue jay), was the first European naturalist to describe—and name—many coastal birds and animals. In 1741 he was the first European biologist ever to lay eyes on Alaska.

The reason Stellers are called sea lions is that they have a way of roaring like land lions. They also share a lion-like tawny color. That, however, is where the similarity ends, except that, like an African lion, the Great Bear Sea Steller sea lion appears kingly. The biggest males weigh up to 1,125 kilograms (almost 2,500 pounds) and can be 3.25 meters (10 feet 6 inches) long, making them far bigger than either a lion or the Great Bear Rainforest's dry-land monarch, the grizzly. About twenty million years ago grizzlies evolved from pinnipeds like sea lions. If you doubt that, compare a sea lion's head to a grizzly's and you'll recognize a kinship. Their growls are similar too.

Also like grizzlies, sea lions can be pretty nasty. When bulls collide during mating season, they'll roar, bark, hiss and bang into each other—like a pair of WWE wrestlers. They'll even wound each other, and judging by the number of scars an old sea lion will carry, it happens fairly often. Females get into the act too.

While males scrap over mates, females will bite, push and threaten each other for breeding grounds. But once a breeding map has been drawn—every combatant to his or her corner—the fights end and peace reigns. At least until next year.

Sea lions are devoted moms, however. Again like grizzlies. They suckle their young well into the pup's second, even third year. Not for them the harbor seal's tough-love boot out the door at only six weeks.

Once a source of blubber, fur and not much else, seals and sea lions are now recognized as important species in the Great Bear Sea, and the sounds of their barks fill the air as they regain old rookeries and haulouts along the coast.

TOP: **A baby sea lion pup will continue to nurse from its mother for one to three years.**

MARITIME MORSELS

Why do seals and sea lions have whiskers?

In 2010 a team of German scientists discovered that a pair of harbor seals named Henry and Nick used their whiskers to detect the very subtle water movements—known as hydrodynamic trails—that fleeing fish leave in their wake. They determined that Henry's and Nick's whiskers were sensitive enough to detect the hydrodynamic trails of herring up to 180 meters, or 600 feet, away. The scientists reckoned these trails caused the seals' whiskers to vibrate in a way that told the seals that dinner wasn't far off.

RIGHT: **A group of Steller sea lions rests on a rocky islet along a proposed oil tanker route in the Great Bear Sea. If an oil spill were to occur in such a pristine place, the sea lions' chances of surviving it would be slim to nil.**

CHAPTER SEVEN
Slippery When Wet

Dolphins and porpoises; porpoises and dolphins. We may have a hard time telling them apart, but we love them all the same. They're like jesters of the sea the way they glide and leap and cavort. No wonder people dream of swimming with them.

Forty-one dolphin and porpoise species dance through the world's waves, but only three are found in the Great Bear Sea: the harbor and Dall's porpoises and the Pacific white-sided dolphin. They're unique among dolphin and porpoise species in that they prefer cool water to warm. Evolution has equipped them with a sea-lion-like insulating layer of blubber that keeps their bodies at a steady temperature no matter how cold the surrounding sea might be. And as you now know, the Great Bear Sea can be very cold indeed.

LEFT: **Only three species of dolphins and porpoises are known to cavort through the cool blue waters of the Great Bear Sea. They are the harbor and Dall's porpoises and the Pacific white-sided dolphin, like this one.**

PHOTOGRAPH BY BRAD HILL

MARITIME MORSELS

What's the difference between a porpoise and a dolphin?

Porpoises are smaller and stockier than dolphins, and they tend to live shorter lives. They also lack the prominent beaks dolphins have, and the single fin on their backs—what biologists call a dorsal fin—is shaped like a triangle. A dolphin's dorsal fin is curved like a horn. Their teeth are different too. Porpoise teeth are flat and cone-shaped; dolphin teeth are pointy.

As the previous chapter explained, pinnipeds, or seals and sea lions, are able to haul out onto islands, reefs or outcroppings to rest, breed and take a break from marauding sharks and killer whales. Not so dolphins and porpoises. Their bodies simply aren't built for locomotion on land. If they become stranded on terra firma, they become, as the saying goes, like a fish out of water. Helpless. So they and their larger cousins, the whales, can't ever leave the ocean. Thus, when a predator appears and the chase is on, speed and stealth are their only means of defense and escape.

Science has a collective name for the world's whales, dolphins and porpoises: *cetaceans*. And all cetaceans—big or small, whale, dolphin or porpoise— share certain characteristics. For one, their tail flukes (flipper-like tail ends) lie in a horizontal plane, parallel to the sea's surface. Fish tail fins lie in a vertical plane, perpendicular to the line of the sea. So when cetaceans slap their flukes, they slap them flat.

They also move their bodies up and down to propel themselves forward. Fish move theirs side to side. Cetaceans use their flukes and the muscles in the hind parts of their bodies to drive themselves forward in the same way we use our legs and feet to swim. They also have a single dorsal fin, triangular or curved, on their backs and two fins attached to their chest muscles that they use for steering and balance.

Cetaceans don't have ears, but they do have strong eyes—the better to see underwater with— and nostrils, called *blowholes*, atop their heads. This makes sense because as mammals they breathe air, so the best place for their noses—those blowholes—is on

the part of their bodies that's exposed first and longest to the atmosphere.

They also have large brains. In fact, some cetacean brains are bigger than human brains. This suggests cetaceans are very intelligent. Certainly they appear that way. What's important to note, however, is that regardless of their size, cetacean brains are uniquely suited to the creatures they serve. So it doesn't make sense to compare animal brains to human brains as indicators of intelligence. It also doesn't do them any favors.

Cetacean bodies, especially whale bodies, are big. But the biggest Pacific white-sided dolphin is no peanut either. They can grow to be 2.5 meters (8 feet) long and weigh more than 200 kilograms or

TOP: **Porpoises and dolphins propel themselves through water by moving their bodies up and down. They also use their flukes (their tail fins) and the muscles in their hindquarters to drive themselves forward— something that comes in awfully handy when they're chasing prey.**

TOP: **How and why Pacific white-sided dolphins returned to the Great Bear Sea is another of nature's mysteries. Between 1915 and 1984 there were none on the BC coast. Then in the early 1980s they began to return. Now they can be found traveling in groups of over a thousand individuals.**

PHOTOGRAPH BY ROB WILLIAMS

440 pounds. But carrying around a big body at sea is much easier than it is on land. When you live on land, gravity makes shifting weight challenging—like weightlifters lifting a barbell. In water (and especially salt water) it's easier because of the water's buoyancy. This is true for animals too. They can grow a lot bigger in water than they can on land. That's why the world's largest marine creature, the blue whale, is so much bigger than the world's largest land animal, the elephant. Elephants have to defy gravity every time they lift a foot; blue whales have the whole Pacific Ocean to hold them up.

A hundred years ago the Great Bear Sea was a very different place because there were so few marine mammals in it. Hunting did away with most humpback whales, sea otters and northern fur seals, but dolphins were few as well. Even as recently as thirty years ago, you wouldn't have seen a Pacific white-sided dolphin, because there were none. Teeth from long-ago dolphins were found in ancient First Nations *middens*, or garbage dumps, meaning they must have been present back then, but from 1915 to 1984 there were none around. And then one day in late 1984, seven were spotted near a group of islands called the Broughton Archipelago. Suddenly and miraculously they were back. And for the next few winters, though only in winter, they kept coming back.

By 1992 there were hundreds of them, and instead of disappearing again when spring arrived, they stayed. And they've remained ever since. The riddle is what brought them back. Scientists suggest it may have been a combination of changing ocean temperatures and the reappearance of such small fish species as capelin, sardines and pilchards, all of which dolphins eat. No one knows for sure, just as no one knows how many Pacific white-sided dolphins there are in the Great Bear Sea today, but the largest pod reported so far contained almost 6,000 individuals.

When we imagine dolphins leaping, jumping and having what looks like a ball, we may not have a particular dolphin in mind, but the Pacific white-sided dolphin fits the bill nicely. Named for its distinctive white sides, almost like panels on a minivan, this dark gray cetacean is among the most playful and gregarious of all marine mammals. They appear to jump simply for the pleasure of it. They'll also ride the bow waves that boats generate and follow in their wakes. And because dolphins are naturally curious,

MARITIME MORSELS

What have pigs got to do with porpoises?

When porpoises were first named thousands of years ago, they were dubbed *porcus piscis*, which in Latin means "pig fish." Britons and Newfoundlanders saw pigs in porpoises too. In parts of Britain porpoises were called "herring hogs," while in Newfoundland they were christened "puffing pigs."

they'll swim for miles to check out a boat traveling through their territories.

They also appear to like the company of other animals. Within the Great Bear Sea they sometimes spend time with Steller sea lions, Dall's porpoises, humpback whales and even resident killer whales. That's not as crazy as it sounds. There are three distinct populations of killer whales off the BC coast—resident, transient and offshore orcas—and the resident population, the dolphins' friends, only eat salmon. (More about them in Chapter Nine.)

Harbor porpoises, as their name suggests, are usually found close to shore. But because of their small dorsal fins and the fact that they don't spend a lot of time near the ocean's surface, they can be tricky to see. Added to that, and unlike show-offy dolphins, they're

BOTTOM: **Herring is a favourite food of the white sided dolphin.**

shy of people and boats. And they hardly ever jump out of the water. No look-at-me "aquabatics" for them. So it's possible that they may be around a lot more than we realize; we just can't see them. Nevertheless, they do make regular appearances in the many inlets, bays and fjords of the Great Bear Rainforest, where they forage for herring, eelpouts, hake, sand lance, salmon, cod, squid and other small fish.

Harbor porpoises are smaller than Pacific white-sided dolphins, growing to no more than 2 meters (6 feet) in length and about 60 kilograms (about 132 pounds) in weight. But they exhibit similar coloring—dark gray along their backs and sides with a white or whitish gray belly. So if you didn't know better, you might mistake one for the other. The difference is that they don't have a dolphin's grinning beak or its curved, horn-like dorsal fin.

TOP: **Unlike harbor seals, harbor porpoises like these ones don't spend a lot of time near the ocean's surface, so they can be difficult to see. But that doesn't mean they're not there.**

PHOTOGRAPH BY BILL CURTSINGER/ NATIONAL GEOGRAPHIC STOCK

TOP: **Unlike the shy and retiring harbor porpoise, Dall's porpoises are as playful as puppies. They even appear to appreciate the shouts and cheers of people admiring them from the decks of ships.**

PHOTOGRAPH BY MIRAY CAMPBELL

The Dall's porpoise got its name from American zoologist William Healey Dall, who lived from 1845 to 1927 and was among the first white men to explore the interior of Alaska. While working as a quartermaster for an American whaler named Charles Scammon, Dall became the first person of European descent to collect a specimen of the porpoise that now bears his name. Dall's porpoises are slightly larger than harbor porpoises and mostly black in color. Like the Pacific white-sided dolphin, they have a distinct white paneling on their sides and bellies too.

Also like dolphins, and unlike their retiring harbor cousins, they're playful. They even engage with ships. They'll leap out of the water, dart and zigzag, and put on quite a show for anyone on board. In fact, Dall's porpoises are thought to be among the fastest cetaceans on Earth, capable of zipping through an ocean wave at speeds up to fifty-five kilometers (thirty-four miles) an hour. That's just slightly above the speed limit of most North American cities. They move so powerfully through water that, like boats, they leave a spray of white water in their wake. Scientists call this spray a "rooster tail," and it is the reason Dall's porpoises are sometimes called "spray porpoises."

However, Dall's porpoises—and their tails—can be difficult to see because they only like deep water, meaning they spend most of their time in open sea. Nevertheless, they are seen quite frequently in the near-shore waters of the Great Bear Sea, so visitors to the forest should keep an eye out for them too.

MARITIME MORSELS

Why do harbor porpoises sometimes strand themselves on beaches?

Scientists don't know, though it may have something to do with how sensitive they are to disturbances. All cetaceans rely on sonar-like systems to tell them where they are and how to find prey. Using a process called *echolocation*, they emit a series of high-pitched, high-frequency sounds that bounce off other objects in the water. When the sound waves return to the porpoise, the porpoise knows where the object is. But with loud ships and seismic testing causing so much noise underwater, cetaceans can become disoriented, and even suffer brain damage. And that's bound to upset their behavior.

LEFT: **It's easy to look at a map of the Great Bear Rainforest and see nothing but green. But without the blue that merges with it along every inch of its coastline, the rainforest simply wouldn't exist.**

CHAPTER EIGHT
Giants of the Deep

Long ago, mythmakers spun stories about sirens. Sirens were creatures that lived in the sea, and the songs they sang were so beautifully seductive that they tempted sailors away from their duties. The great fifteenth-century Italian painter and inventor Leonardo da Vinci once wrote in his notebook: "The siren sings so sweetly that she lulls the mariners to sleep; then she climbs upon the ships and kills the sleeping mariners."

But what exactly were sirens? Scientists suggest that they may have been humpback whales: 15-meter long (or longer), 36,000-kilogram (or heavier) dark gray (or slate blue) animals with large heads, long knobbly flippers, swept-back tail flukes, a humped back (hence their name) and a "blow" (the spray of

LEFT: **The Great Bear Sea could just as easily be called the Great Whale Sea thanks to the many humpbacks (like this one) who now populate its waters during the spring, summer and fall.**

water that comes out of a whale's blowhole) that from certain angles resembles a heart.

And like sirens, humpbacks sing songs, which, to the human ear, sound rather mournful, plaintive and other-worldly. So much so that they once caused the crew of a nineteenth-century British whaling ship to desert their vessel for fear it was haunted.

Why humpbacks sing is a mystery. What we do know is that only males sing (so much for stories about sirens being female) and that they sing mainly at breeding time, which in a humpback's year is winter. This suggests it may have something to do with finding a mate or charting a territory. Though they've also been known to sing while traveling and foraging. And like our music, humpback songs can be very precise. We know this because humpbacks living

BOTTOM: **One of the most memorable sights you'll ever see in the Great Bear Sea is that of a humpback whale "saluting" you with its tail fins, or flukes.**

thousands of kilometers apart will learn exactly the same songs. Scientists are still trying to understand how this is possible.

Before the first industrial whaling ships arrived in the Great Bear Sea more than two hundred years ago, the north Pacific—in fact, the entire Pacific—teemed with humpbacks and other whales. There were blues, grays, seis and fins, to name just a few, all feeding and breeding in an ocean where they were kings— and queens. That is, until human beings arrived with their ships, harpoons and appetites for whale oil.

Thousands were slaughtered over the next two centuries. In many places almost none were left. In 1986, when people finally woke up to the terrible toll whaling had taken, the International Whaling Commission imposed a worldwide *moratorium* (ban) on all commercial whaling. But even today more than a thousand are killed each year by Japanese, Norwegian and Icelandic sailors under the guise of so-called scientific whaling, which they claim they undertake for research purposes.

Yet thanks to that 1986 ban and, more important, to a growing public revulsion for killing whales, some species are coming back. Humpbacks are once again a common spring and summer sight in the Great Bear Sea. Some even remain over the winter. If you're lucky, you also might see a fin or sei whale. Sei whales were once one of the most abundant whales on the BC coast, but more than 61,000 were killed between 1947 and 1987, and today they are exceedingly rare. If you really hit the jackpot, however, you may see a blue whale, the largest animal ever to have lived. Farther out,

MARITIME MORSELS

What other great whales live in the Great Bear Sea?

About a third of all seventy cetacean species known to scientists have been observed at one time or another in the northeast Pacific. They include sei whales, fin whales, minke whales, pilot whales, sperm whales, beluga whales and blue whales.

MARITIME MORSELS

How big is a blue whale?

Huge. They can be 30 meters or 100 feet long (that's two large trailer trucks parked end to end) and weigh up to 180,000 kilograms (200 tons). Their tongues alone can weigh as much as an elephant, and their hearts as much as a car. But the most amazing thing about blue whales is that they attain this gargantuan size by eating nothing but tiny shrimp-like creatures called krill—up to 3,600 kilograms (4 tons) of them each and every day during the spring, summer and fall.

gray whales are a reliable sight each spring and summer as they migrate to and from their feeding grounds in the Bering Sea and their calving grounds in Mexico.

But during the summer, humpbacks reign supreme. Thanks to a worldwide humpback hunting ban imposed in 1968, there are now thought to be about 40,000 around the globe, a far cry from the estimated 240,000 who traversed the seven seas in pre-whaling days, but enough to get themselves noticed. Which is why, if you visit the Great Bear Sea in summer, there's a very good chance that you'll see a humpback…or three. Even ten.

The word *whale* comes from the old English root *hvael* meaning "wheel." This makes sense when you consider that when we observe whales at sea all we usually see of them are the curves of their backs—like the curve of a wheel—as they arc through the waves.

This is certainly true of humpbacks, who use their fore flippers to steer and their flukes—those gigantic tail flippers—to propel them up, down and forward. They also appear to like showing their flukes off, because one of the behaviors humpbacks enjoy most is *tail lobbing*, where they bring their flukes out of the water and then slap them hard on the surface. *Whack!* Tail lobbing also provides scientists with a way to tell humpbacks apart because the white markings on the undersides of their flukes are never the same in any two animals. So recognizing these distinctive markings—like barcodes or fingerprints—is the best way scientists have to tell one humpback from another.

Humpbacks also indulge in something called *spy hopping*, which means holding the top third of their bodies out of the water like a periscope. Which may be why they do it—to get a good look at the lay of the land…or water.

But every now and then humpbacks do something spectacular. With a force that only a whale can muster, they hurl themselves out of the water as if they wanted to fly. First they swim to the surface like a torpedo. Then they jet out of the water like a missile so that for a split second or two it looks as if they're balancing on the points of their flukes. Sometimes just one. Then they fall back with a great whale of a splash. This is called *breaching*. When it comes to chronicling the truly magnificent sights of nature, few compare with that of a great whale throwing itself toward heaven. But if you happen to

TOP: **The Great Bear Sea is home to one of the most significant populations of humpback whales in the world. Take a boat out in the spring or summer and there's a chance that one will stop to greet you.**

PHOTOGRAPH BY BRAD HILL

be in the right place at the right time, you can see it in the Great Bear Sea.

Winter is rarely that time because during December, January and February, after the fall salmon have entered the rivers to spawn and snow has started to fall, most humpbacks abandon the Great Bear Sea for Hawaii or Mexico. Incredibly, these great whales stop feeding in winter, and instead spend their days giving birth, singing new songs and raising their calves before turning around and heading back to the fish-rich waters of the northeast Pacific. So just like grizzlies in their dens, wintering humpbacks feed off their fat. It's only when they return to the Great Bear Sea—a good deal skinnier than when they left—that they eat again.

And what they eat are plankton, krill and schools of small fish that plankton attract. When you consider

BOTTOM: **The sight of a great whale hurling itself toward heaven, or breaching, is one of the most magnificent in all nature.**

PHOTOGRAPH BY BRAD HILL

how small plankton are, it's difficult to imagine that there are enough of them to feed not just one whale, but thousands. Whales that at their biggest can be almost 18 meters (58 feet) long and weigh 40,000 kilograms (45 tons), the equivalent of six and a half African elephants. But that's how abundant plankton and other small life forms are in the Great Bear Sea. Like the forest itself, there's more life in that sea—and more variety of life—than we can ever appreciate.

Humpbacks feed by taking in huge mouthfuls of water, filtering it out through openings in their mouths, and then swallowing whatever food is left. They accomplish this using a system of very narrow plates in their mouths called *baleen*. These baleen plates are made of keratin, like your fingernails, so they're harder than skin, but softer than bone. Each plate, which hangs from the roof of the whale's mouth, is overlaid with a carpet of delicate hairs that trap microscopic plankton and hold on to it. So when the whale expels the water, each of his baleen plates remains covered with thousands of tiny bits of organic matter—those plankton, krill and small fish—that the whale scrapes clean with his tongue and swallows. When a blue whale feeds this way, he can eat up to 3,400 kilograms (4 tons) at one go.

Humpbacks can also sense things underwater thanks to their highly developed hearing. Being able to see clearly underwater isn't much help to a sea-going creature since light becomes scarce the deeper one swims. But being able to hear clearly is a huge advantage because the sea is a very noisy place. The famous French oceanographer and explorer Jacques Cousteau

MARITIME MORSELS

What is the smallest baleen whale?

The minke. They are rarely more than 10 meters (30 feet) long and seldom weigh more than 3,650 kilograms (4 tons). That's still big—as big as the biggest African elephant—but when it comes to size, whales are in a class all their own. When whaling ships were busy slaughtering the world's great whales, the minkes' size worked to their advantage. For a long time, they were thought to be too small to kill. Unfortunately that's changed. Today minke whales are often targeted by Japanese, Norwegian and Icelandic fleets that conduct so-called scientific whaling.

MARITIME MORSELS

How do whales reproduce?

Female whales usually become pregnant sometime between spring and fall. A whale's gestation period is long, anywhere from nine months to a year. Some carry their calves for as long as sixteen months. Most whales give birth to a single calf at a time, though twins are not unknown. And calves are big. A blue whale calf can measure 7 meters (23 feet) in length and weigh up to 7,000 kilograms (8 tonnes). That makes them the biggest newborns in the world.

called it a "vast echo chamber" whose "inhabitants are constantly bombarded with noise." That makes being able to hear well underwater a real gift. In fact, it's believed that because sound travels so far and fast underwater, blue whales were once able to communicate with each other halfway around the world!

Whales have no outer ears like ours; instead they have tiny ear openings behind their eyes. But these ear openings lead to a very sophisticated hearing apparatus in their heads, which they use to locate objects underwater in the same way we locate objects using sight.

How humpbacks feed depends on the humpback. Like bears, each one appears to have its own special technique. But essentially it involves locating sites where large numbers of potential prey have congregated and then sucking that prey up like a fisherman with his net.

One of the most interesting and cleverest ways humpbacks fish is via the bubble net method. A group of humpbacks swimming along the ocean's surface will suddenly dive all at once. Then, when they're underwater, one will begin blowing bubbles from his blowhole while the others begin singing and herding the fish toward the bubbles. Gradually the bubble blower will swim in a circle, making enough bubbles to produce a curtain around the fish. This traps the fish and enables the rest of the humpbacks to scoop them up in their mouths. It's quite a sight when a dozen or so open-mouthed whales break the surface all at once. *Swoosh, splash, gulp, aaah.*

Gray whales were also hunted to near extinction in the nineteenth and early twentieth centuries,

TOP: **Whales breathe through blowholes on the tops of their heads. When they exhale, they can send forth a plume of water like a geyser. Hence the old maritime expression, "Thar she blows!"**

but they, too, have made an impressive comeback. Now there could be as many as twenty thousand of these 40,000-kilogram giants in the northeast Pacific. They've become so reliably visible that whale-watching expeditions all but promise regular sightings, providing it's the right time of year. The best way to know if a gray is close is to watch for the fountain-like sprays they emit from their blowholes. Grays typically blow every ten or twenty seconds when they're resting, so these blows are often the first things whale watchers see. Maybe you've heard the expression "Thar she blows." That's where it comes from.

Like humpbacks, grays winter in the south, off the coast of Mexico, where it's warm. That's also where they mate and bear young. But come spring, they head north again, traveling all the way to the Bering Sea, a journey of more than 8,000 kilometers (5,000 miles). But many stop in the Great Bear Sea to rest and feed on the prodigious amounts of marine life.

Grays, too, have their own unique feeding system, which some observers liken to running a vacuum cleaner along the sea floor. The sea's alternately muddy and sandy bottom is chock-a-block with small animals that grays feast on—as many as three thousand per square foot. To get at them, grays dive to the floor (they can stay underwater for as long as twenty minutes) and turn on their sides. Then, using their powerful flukes to drive themselves forward, it's full steam ahead, their massive mouths open like suitcases.

Most grays swim on their right sides, but a few swim on their left, in the same way that most people are right-handed, but a few are left-handed. No one knows why. But left- or right-sided, in five months they can eat a mind-boggling 54,500 kilograms (60 tons) of food. That's the equivalent of forty-five mid-sized cars. This is also when, like a grizzly bear preparing for winter, a gray whale will amass more than 30 percent of its body weight.

But it's not just grays who benefit from this feeding technique. Seabirds do too. When whales churn up the sea floor, they send plumes of mud to the surface—mud containing food that seabirds eat. Also, by churning up the floor, they stir up various nutrients that encourage the growth of plankton. So even though it may look as if grays are no better than bulldozers for plowing the sea floor so hungrily, they are, like everything else in nature, part of an intricate web.

RIGHT: On a gray day in the Great Bear Sea, the sight of a humpback whale's flukes—like two hands open in a V—above the water's surface can create one of the most hauntingly beautiful moments a visitor could ever enjoy.

CHAPTER NINE

Wolves of the Sea

K iller whales. If ever a name was poisoned by prejudice, this is it. Even if you knew nothing about killer whales, the word *killer* would put you off. A *killer* whale? That has to be a bad thing.

Certainly that's how Europeans and Americans regarded them for centuries. The Roman scholar Pliny wrote way back in the first century AD: "A killer whale cannot be properly depicted or described except as an enormous mass of flesh armed with savage teeth." In 1874, Charles Scammon, a noted nineteenth-century American whaler, author and naturalist, observed: "In whatever quarter of the world [killer whales] are found, they seem always intent upon seeking something to destroy or devour." Even as recently as 1973, US Navy manuals warned that killer whales "will attack human beings at every opportunity."

LEFT: **Pods of killer whales, or orcas, are familiar sights in the Great Bear Sea and all along the British Columbia coast.**

MARITIME MORSELS

Do orcas sleep?

When it's time for orcas to rest, they gather together to form a cohesive unit of animals that dives and surfaces together. At this time, they tend to slow down their movements and can remain underwater for longer periods of time. Their diving and surfacing become very regular, almost like breathing. Pods of orcas can rest for up to seven hours at a time, but usually they're up again after two. During the summer, resident orcas spend about three hours a day resting.

But First Nations peoples, including those living within the Great Bear Rainforest, have always regarded killer whales differently. Because First Nations culture teaches people to be a part of nature, not apart from it, they have always respected killer whales for their strength and admired them for their beauty. Members of the Tlingit Nation believe killer whales will never harm human beings. Instead, they think that, as the sea's top custodian, killer whales will bring them gifts of strength, health and food. Members of the Gitga'at Nation respect killer whales so much that some belong to clan of the killer whale, or blackfish, as they also call them. No wonder killer whales have always taken pride of place in First Nations art and carving.

Today we know that killer whales aren't even whales. They are, in fact, very large dolphins. But everything we've learned about them we've learned fairly recently.

It wasn't until 1964 that non-aboriginal British Columbians began to see killer whales in a new light. Until then, if they thought about killer whales at all, they probably thought the only good one was a dead one. But in 1964, a male killer whale, subsequently misnamed Moby Doll, was harpooned, wounded and taken alive to a small pen in Vancouver harbor. He was badly injured and not expected to live. But he hung on for a remarkable eighty-seven days, and it was then that he became an unwitting ambassador for his species. He looked so sad and vulnerable in his jerry-built pen that, slowly, people began to change their minds about killer whales. Maybe, they thought,

TOP: **The sight of an orca in the wild now fills us with awe. Yet it was only fifty or so years ago that they were hunted by the Canadian government because it was thought they ate too many salmon.**

they weren't so vicious after all. Maybe killer whales were worth caring about too.

This represented a sea change in public opinion. Until then, BC fishermen shot killer whales every chance they got. In 1960, the Canadian Department of Fisheries went so far as to plan to massacre dozens of them with a machine gun mounted onshore in Campbell River, a fishing town on the east coast of Vancouver Island.

But thanks to Moby Doll, that changed. Greenpeace, which got its start in Vancouver in 1971, and other conservation groups began urging people to "Save the Whales," not kill them. In 1980, the first commercial whale-watching tours dedicated to observing killer whales in the wild were introduced off Vancouver Island. And the next year, 1981, marked the last time a killer whale would die in a commercial whale hunt.

Today, when we refer to killer whales, we often call them orcas instead, a word derived from *Phorcys*, the Greek god of the underworld. It also means barrel.

And instead of prompting fear and hatred, orcas are now the object of much study and wonder. Tens of millions of dollars are also generated from tourists who are happy to pay for the opportunity to view one in the wild. But there are only a few places in the world where significant populations can be seen with any certainty, and the Great Bear Sea is one of them. (The others are off the coast of southern British Columbia and Washington State, as well as near Antarctica, northern Japan, Iceland, Norway and Alaska.)

BOTTOM: **There are three types of orcas in the Great Bear Sea, the residents, the transients and the offshore orcas. They may look alike to us, but their behaviors are very different and unique to all three.**

Within British Columbia, there are three distinct populations of orcas: the residents, the transients and the offshores. They may look the same to a casual observer—orcas are black and white, can be 9 meters (about 30 feet) long (at least the biggest males are), weigh up to 5,000 kilograms (11,000 pounds), and have up to fifty-six very sharp flesh-tearing teeth—but the way each population behaves and lives is markedly different.

Resident orcas, named for their tendency to remain in one geographic area, eat mainly fish, primarily salmon. In fact, wherever schools of salmon go, pods of resident orcas follow. And chinook, or king, salmon are what resident orcas prefer to eat because of their high fat content. Ordinarily, orcas eat about 70 kilograms (150 pounds) of food a day, but if a resident orca is really hungry, it can eat up to 4 percent of its body weight—as much as 180 kilograms (400 pounds)—of fish between sunup and sundown. What resident orcas rarely hunt or eat are marine mammals such as seals and sea lions, which is why you sometimes come across orcas and sea lions swimming side by side. In the Great Bear Sea, this is the closest thing you'll see to a lion lying down with a lamb.

The same can't be said for transient orcas. If you've ever seen film or video of an orca hunting a seal, a sea lion or even a baleen whale (it's not a pretty sight), the orca in question is likely a transient. They are the orcas who truly live up to that "killer whale" moniker.

Offshore orcas are more of a mystery. They get their name from the fact that they're usually observed in the middle of the Pacific (and only occasionally

MARITIME MORSELS

Are orcas bothered by whale-watching tours?

No one knows except the orcas themselves. All we can say with certainty is that the sudden approach of a boat can startle an orca and cause the pod's activities to be disrupted. This is why all whale-watching boats are encouraged to be very discreet when they approach an orca pod. The sound the boats make probably affects the orcas' ability to communicate with each other, so it may also affect their ability to find food. As a result there are now laws in British Columbia that make it an offense to get too close to an orca pod.

MARITIME MORSELS

How many orcas are currently held captive in North American aquariums?

Twenty-three. You can find them in San Diego and Los Angeles, California; San Antonio, Texas; Orlando and Miami, Florida; and Niagara Falls, Ontario. Other captive orcas are in France, Spain, Japan and Argentina. In the wild, female orcas can live as long as fifty years. Males, about thirty. Captive orcas of both sexes can live longer than twenty years, but seldom, if ever, do they live as long as they would in the wild.

in the inshore waters of the Great Bear Sea), where they're now known to prey on sleeper sharks and possibly other shark species too. But few people, other than scientists who discovered them only recently, have ever seen them.

So when we talk about the orcas of the Great Bear Rainforest, we're talking mainly about residents and transients.

There are two populations of residents in British Columbia: the southern residents, who commonly navigate the waters around southern Vancouver Island and the San Juan and Gulf Islands; and the northern residents, who frequent the seas near the top half of Vancouver Island, the central coast of British Columbia and occasionally Alaska. These are the resident orcas you'll see in the Great Bear Sea.

We know resident orcas travel in large pods of ten or more animals, and that these pods comprise several related female orcas and their male and female young. In fact, sons and daughters will remain with their mothers for as long as the mother lives. Consequently, most of what a young resident orca learns on his or her way to adulthood comes from his or her mother, aunt or grandmother. Where they do differ from people is that a resident orca's father plays no role in raising his young. But male residents do help rear their younger siblings as well as their nieces and nephews.

Orcas don't sing the way humpbacks do, but they do vocalize when they hunt or forage for food. As members of the dolphin family, orcas are capable of echolocation, a sonar-like system that enables them to find food without actually seeing it. If they make a

noise like a click or a whistle and the noise bounces off an object—like a fish—and back to them, orcas can figure out the shape and nature of the object.

They also keep in touch this way and alert each other to possible dangers, as well as breakfast, lunch and dinner. To the human ear, orca "conversation" sounds like a series of rapid clicks, whistles, screeches and even screams, but to a resident orca, it's a language. A simple language, but a language all the same.

Transient orcas travel alone or in small groups, usually of five or six. Transient mothers may remain with their offspring for several years or a group of unrelated adult females may choose to travel together. Males travel with their mothers. When the mother dies, the male may join a sister's group, or he may bounce back and forth between one group and another.

TOP: **Resident orcas eat mainly fish and mostly salmon. A single orca can consume up to 4 percent of its body weight in a single day. That's an astonishing 180 kilograms or 400 pounds of fish in just twenty-four hours!**

MARITIME MORSELS

Has an orca ever killed a human being?

Yes. In the relatively recent past, three humans have been killed by orcas, but all three orcas were captive animals. By contrast, there has never been a documented killing of a human by a wild orca. The most recent death occurred at SeaWorld in Orlando in 2010 when a male orca named Tilikum pulled a trainer underwater and drowned her. Tilikum also was involved in the death of another trainer in Victoria, British Columbia, in 1991. That trainer slipped and fell into the orca pool after a show, and Tilikum and two female orcas held her down until she drowned. Shortly after that, Sealand, the Victoria facility where Tilikum lived, closed and its orcas were relocated to other aquariums. In 2009 a trainer in Tenerife in Spain was crushed to death by a captive orca named Keto.

And unlike resident orcas, transients move in unpredictable ways. However, because a transient orca's diet consists mainly of marine mammals, it isn't unusual to spot them in the many bays, coves and channels of the Great Bear Rainforest searching for seals (about half a transient orca's diet consists of harbor seals), sea lions, dolphins and porpoises.

Just like people, transient orcas seem to know that the best way to catch something to eat is to sneak up on it. Hence it isn't unusual for transient orcas to dive under the sea's surface—they can hold their breath up to fifteen minutes—so they can shadow their targets like submarines. Then with all the stealth and violence of a ninja, they'll spring into action, taking down a large seal or sea lion the way a lion takes down a zebra. Transient orcas are also very good at hunting cooperatively. A group will trap a dolphin or porpoise in a bay, or harry a large species like a minke to the point that it's too weak to escape or fight back. They are, in other words, true killer whales.

RIGHT: **The killer whale comes by its name honestly. Transient killer whales will kill seals and sea lions as part of their daily diets. It's no wonder these sea lions have decided to clamber onto land.**

CONCLUSION

What Next?

There was a time, not long ago, when humans feared the ocean. And with good reason. We know so little about the underwater world, and being in a small boat on a vast sea can be a very intimidating experience.

Today, however, the sea has much more to fear from humans than the other way around. Because today, and for the first time in our history, we have the power to change the sea. In fact, many scientists warn that the process is already under way, thanks to pollution, overfishing and especially climate change.

We know the ocean is crucial to all life on Earth. That's why many people say we shouldn't call our home "Planet Earth," but "Planet Ocean." Yet Canada, which has the longest coastline in the world, has—so far—protected less than 1 percent

LEFT: **As the sun rises on a cold winter morning, a sea star moves into deeper water during a falling tide.**

MARITIME MORSELS

What is the worst oil spill in North American history?

When British Petroleum's *Deepwater Horizon* oilrig blew up in the Gulf of Mexico in April 2010, it killed ten people and released approximately five million barrels of oil into the surrounding ocean. It's still impossible to calculate the long-term damage done to the environment and human health given that studies are still being conducted. The worst oil spill in history occurred during the 1991 Gulf War when Iraqi forces deliberately opened the valves of a number of oil wells and pipelines in an attempt to slow the invading coalition forces. As a result, some 910 million liters, or 240 million gallons, of crude oil flowed into the Persian Gulf.

of its marine environment. This is what needs to change—and quickly.

It is an urgent race against time, and time is running short. But fortunately, as we learn more about the ocean and the species that live there, the more we are working on solutions to ensure its survival.

It is still possible to turn things around. There was a time not long ago when governments and logging companies refused to protect more than 12 percent of the land portion of the Great Bear Rainforest. At first the situation seemed hopeless; they refused to budge or compromise. But the people who loved the rainforest refused to give up. Scientists, First Nations and countless other concerned individuals from around the world—people like you—who wanted more of the rainforest protected, slowly changed the logging companies' and the governments' positions. Because of those efforts, more than 30 percent of the Great Bear's trees are now protected, and work is ongoing to protect even more.

Today the most immediate threat facing the Great Bear Sea is from a proposed oil pipeline that would run from Alberta to Kitimat, a port within the Great Bear Rainforest. There, the oil would be transferred to tankers, each one longer than two football fields, which would deliver the oil to Asia and the United States. The potential for a big oil spill is immense, and the consequences of such a spill would be catastrophic. Who knows how long it would take the sea to recover—if ever?

But people opposed to the pipeline are making themselves heard. Despite the vocal support of the

Government of Canada, it's no longer certain that the pipeline will be built. Too many people have stood up and said, "No."

If there is one place on our planet that we can and must protect, it's the ocean. Our own survival depends on it. And it is never too early to begin. Working together to make the right decisions and take the right actions will make all the difference. As long as we do that, there's no reason why the Great Bear Sea won't remain wild and wet and teeming with life for years to come. It all depends on us.

TOP: **The single largest and most immediate threats to the Great Bear Sea are the enormous tanker ships that the Canadian government would like to see transport oil and gas from the Great Bear Sea to Asia. If oil ports are built and tankers start to use them, acoustic disturbance and spills will happen, and wildlife and human communities will suffer. Nevertheless, there is still time to protect this one-of-a-kind coastal paradise.**

FOR MORE INFORMATION

Have you been inspired by the Great Bear Sea? If so, maybe you would like to join the growing effort to protect it. Pipelines and tankers, oil spills and overfishing, should not be part of the Great Bear Sea's future. If this pacific paradise is going to have a safe future, now is the time to add your voice.

Pacific Wild is a non-profit conservation organization that works to protect wildlife in this important coastal wilderness. Pacific Wild supports innovative research, public education, community development, and global awareness to achieve the goal of lasting wildlife protection. A portion of the royalties earned from the sale of this book will support Pacific Wild's work.

For more information on the Great Bear Sea or to learn how to support Pacific Wild's conservation work please contact us at:

Pacific Wild
PO Box 26, Denny Island, BC
V0T 1B0, Canada

WEBSITE: www.pacificwild.org
FACEBOOK: www.facebook.com/PacificWild.org
EMAIL: info@pacificwild.org

Visit www.GreatBearSea.com and download the Great Bear Sea video.

OTHER SUGGESTED READING

Cannings, Richard and Sydney Cannings. *British Columbia: A Natural History*. Vancouver: Douglas & McIntyre, 1996.

Cannings, Richard, Sydney Cannings and Marja de Jong Westman. *Life in the Pacific Ocean*. Vancouver: Greystone Books, 1999.

Lamb, Andy and Bernard P. Hanby. *Marine Life of the Pacific Northwest: A Photographic Encyclopedia of Invertebrates, Seaweeds and Selected Fishes*. Madiera Park: Harbour Publishing, 2005.

McAllister, Ian. *The Last Wild Wolves: Ghosts of the Great Bear Rainforest*. Vancouver: Greystone Books, 2007.

McAllister, Ian and Karen McAllister. *The Great Bear Rainforest: Canada's Forgotten Coast*. Madeira Park: Harbour Publishing, 1997.

McAllister, Ian and Nicholas Read. *The Salmon Bears: Giants of the Great Bear Rainforest*. Victoria: Orca Book Publishers, 2010.

McAllister, Ian and Nicholas Read. *The Sea Wolves: Living Wild in the Great Bear Rainforest*. Victoria: Orca Book Publishers, 2010.

Morton, Alexandra. *Listening to the Whales: What Orcas have Taught Us*. New York: Ballantine Books, 2004.

Vernon, Caitlyn. *Nowhere Else on Earth: Standing Tall for the Great Bear Rainforest*. Victoria: Orca Book Publishers, 2011.

ABOUT THE ARTIST

An artist from childhood, Martin Campbell depicts scenes of his daily life and Heiltsuk culture in his work.

INDEX

Page numbers in **bold** refer to photographs.

Also by *Ian McAllister* and *Nicholas Read:*

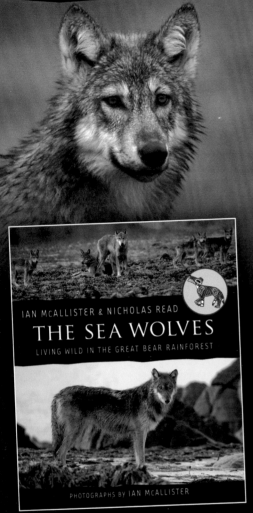

9781554692064 • $19.95 paperback with flaps
Full-color photos • Ages 8+

"[An] engaging account...Augmented by a bounty of sharp photos taken at close range (that say as much about this stunning section of the Pacific coast as they do about the wolves)...the authors provide a comprehensive study." —*Publishers Weekly*

"This extensive, informative text is illustrated with remarkable photographs taken by McAllister...They show the lush, old-growth forest and rocky shoreline and a variety of animals that share this habitat, but the wolves are the stars: at rest, at play, on the prowl and catching fish...Fascinating and useful." —*Kirkus Reviews*

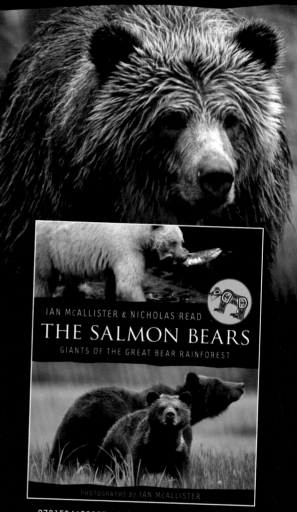

9781554692057 • $18.95 paperback with flaps
Full-color photos • Ages 8+

"This excellent book...[has] a sprightly narrative that takes the reader through a year in the life of a bear...The illustrations for this book, a plentitude of photographs...are nothing short of gorgeous." —*The Globe and Mail*

"Read's conversational text and McAllister's excellent photos provide a perfect framework for this evocative look at...the Great Bear Rainforest of British Columbia, and an intriguing investigation of its ecological pattern of dependency... Superbly readable, informative, and attractive, this book provides a clear picture of a pristine environment and its major inhabitants." —*School Library Journal*

WWW.SEAWOLVES.CA › WWW.SALMONBEARS.COM

2/11

D0702222

Gay People of Color: Facing Prejudices, Forging Identities

The Gallup's Guide to Modern Gay, Lesbian, & Transgender Lifestyle